Acclaim for Carol's book

"In *Single Smiling Mom*, Carol takes us on her personal journey through not one but two of life's larger emotional, physical hurdles. She does so by showing acceptance of self, appreciation of the simple things in life (family, friends, nature, and food). A delightful book yet heartfelt leaving you the reader with many opportunities to reflect..."
~ Don Ely, author of *Forgive and Let Go* and
   Lead Engineer at ERC Kennedy Space Center

"A deeply vulnerable, incredibly insightful and beautifully written journey of one courageous woman's transformational journey through fear to love. Dive in and allow Carol's words to uplift you, inspire you and ultimately enlighten you!"
~ Laurel Geise, author of *The Jesus Seeds: Igniting Your Soul-Guided Life.*

"Beautiful... Wonderful...amazing and inspiring...as I finished the last pages I started to feel like it can't be over...it's just beginning... And in saying that realized what a profound meaning that has and it has resonated for me in my own life after reading these words of yours. I feel ....I know things... life happens for reasons beyond our knowledge but for our greatest good! This book is proof of that. I feel honoured and blessed to have felt a piece of this with you on this journey we call life."
~ Mindy Grover, Executive Director at Boys and Girls Club of Olds

"This book can change many, many lives... Carol explains simply how one can change the circumstances of our lives. Through a knowing of how the DIVINE Universe works. One can tap into it. Carol herself used this WISDOM to turn her own life around. Everything truly is ENERGY... Even thoughts create. This is now leading edge science... you don't need to know how it works... just BELIEVE it does... let Carol guide you to your happiest life. ☺"
~ Carl Stedmond, Self-Empowerment Coach, Singer/Songwriter

"WOW!! This book is a gift. It is a gift to anyone trying to figure out how to navigate through a world of challenges. Carol's strength in taking control of her body, mind and spirit shows how miracles can happen and through her example, how we can manifest miracles for ourselves. This is a book to be read and re-read whenever the need for inspiration sets in. It will inspire you to live a better life."
~ Sue Methuen, author of ebook *"Manifesting Miracles, Soul Mates & Parking Spots – Real Life Law of Attraction Stories"*

"I love the book. Such an inspiration. God really has a hand in absolutely everything. It made me laugh and cry and just simply smile as I read it. You can't help but see the emotion, joy and beauty in the words that Carol has written. I was blessed to be given an early opportunity to feel what she has chosen to share. Thank you Carol for sharing this with us."
~ Shelly Majore, works at Alberta Health Services

"This beautiful book is unlike any other personal account of living with cancer that I have read AND she does it as a single Mom! Smiling Single Mom changed the way I think about cancer and parenting. This beautifully written book offers patients and families practical insights into how they can live their life more fully and derive meaning from amidst the heartbreak of a body-robbing illness."
~ Janet Almond, business woman and mother

"It is all about telling your story, and hoping that it helps someone else as they travel that same road. I admire your ability to single parent two children while going thru treatments – I am not sure how you did that but I know you will provide inspiration to anyone who reads your story. I hope you gave yourself lots of pats on the back... they seem like great boys."
~ Kimberley Rideout, author of *Taken to my Knees*

Smiling Single Mom

It's ALL Right!

Carol Taylor

BALBOA.
PRESS

A DIVISION OF HAY HOUSE

Artwork by Janice Gallant

Balboa Press books may be ordered through booksellers or by contacting:

Balboa Press
A Division of Hay House
1663 Liberty Drive
Bloomington, IN 47403
www.balboapress.com
1 (877) 407-4847

Because of the dynamic nature of the Internet, any web addresses or links contained in this book may have changed since publication and may no longer be valid. The views expressed in this work are solely those of the author and do not necessarily reflect the views of the publisher, and the publisher hereby disclaims any responsibility for them.

The author of this book does not dispense medical advice or prescribe the use of any technique as a form of treatment for physical, emotional, or medical problems without the advice of a physician, either directly or indirectly. The intent of the author is only to offer information of a general nature to help you in your quest for emotional and spiritual well-being. In the event you use any of the information in this book for yourself, which is your constitutional right, the author and the publisher assume no responsibility for your actions.

Any people depicted in stock imagery provided by Thinkstock are models, and such images are being used for illustrative purposes only. Certain stock imagery © Thinkstock.

Print information available on the last page.

ISBN: 978-1-5043-3530-0 (sc)
ISBN: 978-1-5043-3531-7 (hc)
ISBN: 978-1-5043-3532-4 (e)

Library of Congress Control Number: 2015909885

Balboa Press rev. date: 6/26/2015

Smiling Single Mom

"Life is all about choices, so make the
ones that 'feel right' for you."
Carol Taylor

I dedicate this book to my boys. I am so blessed to share my life with you. Thank you for being just the way you are. Without you I wouldn't be here now. You gave me the reason to keep going. Know that I will always be there for you. Through whatever ups and downs life hands to you on your journey. May you always have the wind beneath your wings.

I Love You Forever! ☺

Contents

Preface xvii

Welcome xxi

August - FEAR 1

September - GRIEF 2

October - DEPRESSION 10

November - DESPAIR 15

December - POWERLESSNESS 18

January - INSECURITY 22

February - GUILT 24

March - UNWORTHINESS 26

April - JEALOUSLY 29

May - HATRED 31

June - REVENGE 38

July - ANGER 39

August - DISCOURAGEMENT 42

September - BLAME 45

October - WORRY 47

November - DOUBT 50

December - DISAPPOINTMENT 54

January - OVERWELMENT 57

February - FRUSTRATION 59

March - IRRITATION 61

April - IMPATIENCE 63

May - PESSIMISM 66

June - BOREDOM 68

July - CONTENTMENT 70

August - HOPEFULNESS 72

September - ACCEPTANCE..77

October - OPTIMISM 80

November - POSITIVE EXPECTATION 84

December - BELIEF 88

January - ENTHUSIASM 91

February - EAGERNESS...94

March - HAPPINESS..97

April - PASSION 99

May - JOY.. 102

June - EASE... 105

July - APPRECIATION 108

August - EMPOWERMENT.. 111

September - FREEDOM 114

October - INSPIRATION.. 118

November - AWE... 120

December - LOVE.. 122

Thanks for Coming 125

For Your Thoughts.. 127

Acknowledgements.. 129

How To Find Me 133

Recommended Reading Resources....................................... 135

About Carol 137

About Janice.. 139

This painting inspires me. It's a work of art done by Janice Gallant and it's called "Castle Mountain". It's a real mountain in our own majestic Rockies and it is in our nearby Banff National Park. I love Janice's art because it has so much underlying meaning and for me it represents the beauty of it all. When I first looked at this piece I saw the hearts in it right away. There is so much color and energy in her art. This piece, in particular, inspires me because this is where the boys and I play - where we see the rightness of life. For me, mountains represent life. Sometimes we are lower and travel through lush meadows where there is flowing water and often we are confronted with high peaks, uncertainty, unpredictability and storms that can come suddenly. To some they scream impossible but to me they scream "I'm possible". When the boys and I stand on the top of the mountains and look down we see a whole new perspective on life. From up here we become one with the sky, nature and all that is beautiful.

Become the Sky

The cage that you've been trapped inside
for longer than you can remember—
it might seem so sturdy and secure
that you don't even dream of escaping anymore
like a bird that used to beat its wings
but now just lets them hang limply by its side.

But the bars of the cage aren't even solid
They're a mirage made up of fears and desires
projected by your restless mind
fuelled by the attention you give them.

Just for a moment, let your mind be quiet
and see how fears evaporate
see how desires withdraw
like the claws of an animal that's no longer threatened.

Watch the bars melt away
and let the world immerse you
let your mind-space merge with space out there
until there is only space, without distinction—
stretch your wings and become the sky.

From *The Calm Center* by Steve Taylor

Preface

This book is born from my journey through breast cancer as a teacher and as a single mom with two boys, Jaden and Zach. It is a narrative with reflection and contains the rightness of everything. It developed from a compilation of journal entries and Facebook posts which happened over the past three years. I had an intuitive knowing that I was to write a book so I kept all my journals and calendars until now, until I was strong enough to share it. And really, I am thankful for the cancer experience because it was my wakeup call and I learned so much. I hope now that this book helps others who are facing hardship in their lives. It's time for me to give back.

I've had many people say that once they have read my story then something SHIFTS and all of a sudden they start seeing the rightness in everything and when the shift happens more amazing stuff just flows to them. I hope my book helps you to manifest everything beautiful. I invite you to journal, paint or be creative in your own special way, as you read through these pages. Read slowly and stop often and reflect on your own feelings and look for the love, gratitude and happiness that reside in your own heart. Highlight and fold down corners and make this book a learning journey for you. I invite you to do this whenever you feel you want to and I will prompt your creative expression with a reflective question at the end of each section. Honest reflection is the fire of integrity. Inspired people do great things.

We're all on our own unique, individualized journeys within the whole of everything. What do you chose? And how do you see things? What you see will depend on what you are looking for and what you believe. We don't manifest what we want but we manifest what we believe. The Law of Attraction says, "Ask – Believe – Receive". I think that the main step is to Believe. We ask all the time, consciously and unconsciously and we receive all the time, too. The way to focus on your dreams is to Believe. This is where the good stuff happens. When you really believe, then it will happen. For me, I change the "Ask – Believe – Receive" and turn it into "Ask – Align – Allow – Achieve". We ask all the time and we achieve all the time and the good stuff is in the middle. That is where the magic lies for me. I Align with my inner purpose where I feel good, trust, love and know and then I allow the universe to deliver to me all that I have asked for. When I Allow, I let go of resistance, stress and fear. It has worked for me so far, so I will keep doing this.

I like to believe that if you need a helping hand you'll find it at the end of an arm. We have two hands - one to help ourselves and one to help others. Also, when we help others, it in return helps us. What you give out, you get back. A win-win situation! I think that it's good to have a goal/want/desire just as long as we remember that it's the journey that matters in the scheme of things. Also that, we humans make a living by what we get paid but we make a life that is real by what we give to others. It's my belief that life can shrink or expand depending on your generosity and courage. As I wrote this book I discovered that my life could only be understood by looking backwards and then moving forward. I try to spend more time looking forward then back though because when you drive a car your eyes should be on the road, not always in the mirror or you will crash. All life has a message, you just have to listen and learn. I now allow the Universe to yield to me everything that I have put there. When I am on the right path it feels easy and smooth and everything just flows. It feels like it is meant to be. I breathe in calm... I breath out relax, and when I do this, I feel the unconditional love that surrounds me. It's important to do what you love and to love what you do. Everyone has problems. It's how you handle them that counts. You get to choose what you want to see and decide what next step you will take. You have to have a dream and a burning desire to achieve it. Remember to be yourself and to laugh, enjoy, be happy and love. We humans can alter our lives by altering our attitudes. We are deliberate creators and as we think, so shall we be.

My writing came from a place of calmness, stillness and centeredness, a place of flow. I hope that when you read it, you go to that place too. Take a deep breath and another deep breath and feel the stillness that lies within you at this very moment and savor it. Thank you for coming on this journey from 'Fear' to 'Love' with me. I love you and you are the best. Keep Smiling! ☺

Welcome

August 22, 2011 is the day my life took a HUGE turn. Here I am sitting in the medical office. I got a call to come in and see my doctor and as I sit here, it dawns on me that I am the only one in the waiting room. This can't be good! I'm also holding in my hand a piece of paper that says my divorce is final and it's stamped with today's date. This is quite a day!

Breast Cancer? WTF! I'm scared. This has to be a mistake! Nobody in my close family has ever been diagnosed with this! I want to be tested again! I'm paralyzed by fear. I don't know what to do and my panic sets in. My doctor and I cry then we hug and now I need to feel this fear and take the steps that I need to take to get better. I need to focus on good health. First with a thought change… I am surrounded by love and I am grateful for that. I need to remember to breathe deeply because when I'm afraid like this my breathing becomes shallow and I don't get enough oxygen to my brain. I need to focus on 3-4-5. A deep breathe in for three seconds, hold it for four seconds then breathe out for five seconds. Pause and feel the stillness and do it again. Okay, I'm good. This Just Breathe technique has helped me on many occasions as I ventured down the divorce road and started to feel anxiety, panic and fear arising. Here is something for my emotional toolbox. A great resource. Right now, I choose to take one step closer to my goal. My goal is - Abundance in all areas of my life, starting with my health. YES TO SUCCESS!

August - FEAR

August was my month of fear. Fear of what had happened in my past and of the mistakes that I had made in my marriage. Fear of future relationships that may go bad. Fear of the unknown as I was tested for cancer and fear while I waited for the test results. Fear of not knowing what the future holds for the boys and me. Fear of the present moment and of the strange way my body was reacting to stress. Fear of the low grade fever that would come and go. Fear of how weak I was feeling. Fear of how this was going to affect the boys.

Then it donned on me that all this negative self-talk was going to drag me slowly and surely to death and then the fear disappeared and I was left with a calm feeling of knowing that all would be okay, that everything was alright. Here it was, a feeling, a beautiful, calm feeling that the road ahead was uncertain but that somehow it was all going to be okay. I surrendered to it and from that moment on I moved myself up the emotional scale one step at a time. What did I have in my life to focus on that was good? That was right? First and the most important was the boys. Second was the roof over our head. Third was my family and friends. I sat down and wrote about all the beauty in my life and of everything that was right about it. My deep fear launched a powerful rocket of desire to feel better. I had asked. Now it was my job to align and allow so that I could achieve what I had asked for.

Reflect - What fear do you want to acknowledge?

September - GRIEF

Here I am at grief. I am grieving the loss of my old life and all that was familiar to me. I feel a grieving that is deep within my soul. Now I take a step up to see the rightness in this situation and from there I see that within each of us is a gorgeous flower garden called the soul. As we grow and learn the garden grows. As we grow and learn with others our collective garden grows too into a captivating and whole garden.

Journal entry (2nd) - I'm looking for the rightness in the day to day things and I'm finding it everywhere. It is the first day of school for my charming boys. Grade three for Zach and grade nine for Jaden. It's going to be a great year. I spent some time on Facebook this morning reading inspirational quotes, messages and posts. There are so many positive, sharing, caring people out there. The positive vibes I received this morning are bringing me out of fear and back into life. My friend, Gabriel, put the boys and me on a prayer list so people literally around the world are praying for us. Everyone needs a team to achieve great things. I can't do this on my own. Thank you Gabriel for your kindness and caring.

Notes to self... I need lemon, cinnamon and honey and a good positive attitude. I need inner strength/love and a belief in myself. This will lead me to growth, beauty and freedom. I will build an exquisite alter with my pile of rocks. I will plant grass and flowers and put a flag on top (maybe a friendship flag). The beauty will flourish, grow and change and butterflies and bugs will come to signify freedom. The soul is like a flower garden and right now I am in the center and there are flower gardens growing all around me. I am protected and loved and one day I will help plant seeds in the next alter. Oh, and a fountain. Water is very soothing for me! I surround myself with beauty and everything that feels good. Accept and then keep moving forward. By letting go of inner resistance, I find that things change for the better which allows me to see the rightness of all things. Optimism got me through the divorce. This can be done too. Exercise. Drink lots of water. Soul journal. Live – Love – Laugh – Let Go. Feel Good – Give Thanks – Trust. Be aware. Look - Listen - Learn –Lead. Just Breath. I love my Boys. I will do this for you. I will do this for us!

How am I doing? GREAT! Thanks for asking. Yes, I'm in the flow again. I will do whatever it takes to FEEL GOOD NOW. Was this a curve ball? Nope, this is a pile of rocks and I will build a beautiful fountain. I love me and I'm perfect exactly where I am. It's time for some lemon and honey and a ride on my exercise bike. I'm in a place of Love & Trust. The boys are off to school and I'm going grocery shopping soon. As I dropped the boys off at the bus I ran into Jeff, who was outside doing bus supervision. He gave me a hug and reminded me that attitude is everything and to keep it positive. Thanks Jeff! I interpret this situation to be one of great growth and growth is good. It is essential to life. I will be keeping busy today. I have yard work, finances, housework and I'm going out to the farm. A busy body doesn't worry.

Now a tired body needs to read *Fighting Cancer* by Contreras/Kennedy. Every book is a journey and masterpiece unto itself and all who get something from it. From this book I took away that some good foods are fruits/veggies, whole grains, All bran cereal, garlic, grapes, alfalfa, broccoli, berries, carrots, soy, nuts, artichokes, tomatoes, fruit juices, oranges, beans (zinc), oysters, zinc fortified cereals, fatty acids, cocoa, green tea. After reading that, I'm now hungry. This journey has put me completely in the moment. I guess this is part of the learning experience. I also took from the book that I should focus on what makes me happy. Things like exercise, sing, believe, pray (thank you for my healing), laugh and keep stress down. YES! Reduce stress. That is the big one for me! That is my cause. The next book I am going to read is called, *Staying Alive* by Brenda Hunter. It looks like it deals a lot with healing body, mind and soul. Thank you to Diane for lending the book to me.

When I'm stronger I'm going to get a tattoo and it will represent: Love + Trust which leads to Growth, Beauty and Freedom. There will be a red heart, a pink, thorn less rose and a butterfly.

Journal entry (4th) - I feel good this morning. I woke in the night at 1:00 am, did some breathing and a relaxation exercise (tighten and release my muscles one at a time) and then fell back asleep until 6:00. Yes to success! Yesterday we spent the evening at the farm with Wendy & Mike, Janet & Perry, Dad & Irene and all those amazing nieces and nephews. I love my family and I am so blessed. Had such a healing evening that we are going back today for more fresh air, love and exercise. I'm looking forward to an awesome day and another good sleep tonight. This was the best day I have had in a month!

I was walking through the grocery store today and BANG it hits me - a huge rush of emotions! Not even sure what song was playing over the speaker but it set me off. I took a deep breath but it didn't work. It was hard to breathe and I felt like I had a huge weight on my chest. My cart was half full of groceries and I had a desperate need to get out of the store to get myself together. Luckily I was close to the office so I asked the girl if she could keep my groceries until I returned. She saw the tears all over my face and said, "Absolutely". Head down, tears flowing, I half walked and half ran out the front door and then sprinted to my car. I cried it out in my car and felt a lot better.

Thursday I'm off to the specialist in Calgary with Irene and today I faced huge feelings of denial. Something is telling me this is an infection. Please God let them find that out and let it just be an infection. Antibiotics and some rest time. Yes, that would be awesome. What is with this low grade fever that comes and goes? I would be soooo happy to tell the boys that I will be healthy in a few days and that all will be back to normal and that this was just a wakeup call to take care of me and love me.

I went to the football meeting tonight. Sharon asked if the team could wear pink ribbons on the October first game in support of breast cancer awareness month and to show support to Jaden and me. I got tears and goose bumps. Jaden said it would be okay with him. I told him that he has the final say in the matter. We are so blessed and surrounded by love. All will be well. All IS well and is just as it was designed to be. The Universe has great surprises in store for the boys and me. We all get knocked down in one way or another at some time in our lives.

Journal entry (8th) - It's early but I couldn't sleep so I decided to get up and journal and exercise rather than just laying here worrying. Going to ride my exercise bike and listen to inspirational stuff on YouTube while I sip my green tea. I made a video for the boys of our adventures from last summer and it just gets me in the zone when I watch it (https://youtu.be/X_dg-xuFJSY). It helps me to feel the support of family, friends, community and beyond! Thank you for this amazing feeling! I am wrapped in a blanket of love and I trust everything is fine. Bring it on!

Inspired to write. When an experience comes into your life that knocks you down, you may just need to sit there for as long as you need to, and then try to make friends with it. Heed its call. Let it change your life. Slow down. Pay attention. Prioritize. Pace yourself. Respect your body. Spend time with those whose presence is healing. Notice small miracles that happen daily like birds singing, morning air, sunshine on your skin, the smell of a pink rose, the melody of raindrops, the sweetness of a child's smile and hug, the beauty of a sunrise or a sunset, the presence of those you love and who love you. Let love in. Open your heart. Tell the truth. Ask for help. Accept the profound generosity of family and friends. Let whatever you have given, come back to you. Allow it to remind you of what is actually important in life. Have a relationship with it that fosters new insights. See the uninvited experience as an opportunity for learning and growth. Accept the many gifts and joys which life offers. Don't waste time complaining about things you can't change or which you wish were different. Dance and sing when you can. Weep when you must. Notice what you have instead of what you don't have. Practice thoughtfulness and forgiveness. Do not hide from it or hate it but acknowledge it. Accept what it has to teach you and continue on your journey, one step at a time.

Tired tonight. Everything went so fast and flowy-like at the specialists in Calgary. I have to say that when the medical system in Alberta finds something wrong, they move and fast. I have been booked for a mastectomy next Friday the sixteenth. Now I can focus on my healing and keep moving forward. I have two very handsome and important reasons to get better ASAP. All is well. I'm happy where I am and eager for more. Bring it!

I feel so loved and supported but today was still an off day. Very tired and out of sorts and feeling draggy and yucky. I'm guessing that this is probably because of all the excitement that happened yesterday at the specialist. Then as if answering my call for something right to happen, my friend, Val, showed up for a visit. She brought a plant, a *Whole Living* magazine, special juice and chips. We laughed, we cried, we prayed, we chatted. So many people love us. I will sleep well. Thanks Val. My beautiful friend!

It's the middle of September and we went to the football game at Sylvan Lake and I truly appreciated the cool, fresh air and supported feeling I got when I was with my football family. I'm still floating on cloud nine. I sat near Sharon and Nancy and we cheered hard for the boys in the pink laces. Pink Power! This was the first game with the boys wearing the pink laces in their cleats. I High-fived the young men as they entered the football field and I even got a few hugs. It was a thirty two to zero win for the team. They kicked butt and so can I!

Went and took Zach to the bus this morning and Nicola's hugs filled my bucket. It seemed to drain me getting groceries and doing some cleaning. Made sure I rested today for fifteen minutes. After school I was feeling energized so I walked over to get Zach off the bus. Val told me that the Deer Meadow School staff will bring us suppers for two weeks starting the nineteenth. What an awesome surprise. I love my community and the people in it! Thanks for making my day, my amazing school family.

Taking the good with the bad - I had a down day. I rode my exercise bike and cried and cried till there were no more tears. It felt good to just let it all go so that I was able to put on a happy face when the boys woke up. I don't want them to worry or they will be the next ones getting sick. I had to give up my vitamins to prepare for surgery, especially missing my B vitamin. I think that is the reason for the down day. On the upside, Trish came and did a Reiki on me. Thanks Trish. The love flows to me every day through my friends and the boys. Those two are my reason for living. Our little family of three is getting stronger day by day. This is the hardest thing I have ever done and as I face it one day at a time, I get stronger and stronger.

Friends stopped by yesterday, and mom is here today. I get to have breakfast with the boys then hug them off to school. After that, mom and I are going to the city for a sentinel node mapping to prepare for surgery tomorrow. I feel strong. I feel safe. I feel surrounded by a blanket of love. All is well as I take one step at a time and trust. I'm following my impulses and trusting that the path will come to me. Trust + Love = WOW. I know I will not be given more than I can handle.

Surgery went well. Felt great the day of. I vaguely remember the nurses bringing me back to my bed after the surgery and I remember them trying to move me onto the bed. It was uncomfortable as they tried to move me and I remember saying, "I can do it". They stepped back as I wiggled my way from one bed to the other. They were so patient and understanding and as they left with the surgery bed, I heard one of them say, "Yes, she will do it!" and then I focussed on my breathing, 3-4-5. I thought about the boys and I found the place inside where there's joy and I let the joy burn out the pain. Janet, who is my youngest sister, was with me all day and was a great help to me. We laughed, we cried and we hugged and let me tell you laughing is not easy after surgery. We walked around the ward of the hospital with my tall pole buddy and came face to face with another patient who was out for a walk, with his buddy. The halls were not that big and we had to squeeze around each other to continue our walk. Janet looked at me and said "BEEP! BEEP!" I burst out laughing and she had to help balance me so I didn't fall over. Then the nurse came running over and asked Janet if I was alright. Not sure why it was so funny but it was and to this day Janet will text me "BEEP! BEEP!" for no reason but to make me smile and laugh. I also had a nice visit with my friend Tim, who stopped by.

Coming home the next day was good too. I didn't realize how weak I was until I walked into my house and hugged my boys. Wendy, who is my middle sister, drove me home and mom was here too. Mom had spent the night with the boys. I had a grouchy, ouchy day! I think the pain meds had worn off. BEEP! BEEP! didn't work today. I think I was mourning the loss of my right breast. THEN had a nice sleep and am now looking forward to a great day. Some fresh air, a small walk, a shower and this afternoon the gauze bandage comes off. I love my family!

Journal entry (20th) - Mom went home yesterday. The boys and I are doing fine. It is nice to get back to routine. I am inspired by the profound generosity of family, friends and our community. What a beautiful world it is! Jaden has football practice tonight. It will be the first time driving my car since surgery. Also, the drain tubes are almost down to the point where I can have them removed. Maybe tomorrow! Tonight, I am helping Jaden get ready for grade nine camp. He will be gone Thursday and Friday and on Saturday he'll be going to Rocky Mountain House for a football game. Vockeroth's are going to drive him. Zach is happy that things are feeling more normal. I love my boys. Those two amazing young men are my reason for getting healthy. I'll do whatever it takes. They need me and I need them!

I discovered some more things that were right as I rode my exercise bike this morning, slowly, for twenty minutes while on my computer. It felt great! Drain tubes at 26.5 mL output in twenty-four hours. Tomorrow they come out! Standing on my back deck, I am appreciating the sunrise. RADIANT! I took many pictures and I think I will make the prettiest one the cover photo on my Facebook page. It's going to be an awesome day!

Jaden departed for grade nine camp this morning. He is off to make memories and learn and grow. He will be gone until tomorrow at five. I'll miss him. Just a taste of what it will be like when he moves out. Jaden helps in more ways than he even knows. He is there physically if I need help and he is also there emotionally. Sometimes I just have to go into his room and lay on his bed and I feel better. His presence is calming and often words are not even needed. We just have to be in the same room. I'm sure he feels this too. He is my strong, silent boy. Also, another step taken today as I went to the emergency ward at the Olds hospital and had the drains removed. OUCH! But I'm glad they are gone. One week to heal until the follow up appointment. Thank you for my healing!

Moving forward, I had an appointment with my surgeon today. Irene and Wendy came with me. My scar is looking good. I have lots of nerve damage from when they removed the lymph nodes and I have limited movement in my right arm. I'll be going to physiotherapy to get things moving again. Everything looks good for lymphedema. They got the pathology report back from the lymph nodes that were removed and the cancer had spread into the lymph system. She is concerned, also, about the margin around the tumor itself because they removed all they could without cutting into the chest muscle. The course of action will be six rounds of chemo, three weeks apart, followed by radiation and five years of the drug Tomoxafin. That is a lot to swallow for one day. I'm going home to hug my boys.

Reflect - When was there a time that you felt grief and did you find love and wisdom from it?

October - DEPRESSION

This month I dipped in and out of feelings of depression. The good news is that I am becoming very aware of my feelings and how they are affecting me. This sadness and stress was impacting my physical health. My emotions were triggering chemical reactions in my body which were weakening my immune system. So although there were occasional feelings of depression I could catch them early before they gained momentum and carried my body and mind down further.

The Bulldogs played Strathmore, a couple days ago, in Olds. The football boys wore the pink ribbons tied around their arms and legs. Mom came and watched the game with me. It felt good to be back with my football family. I had physiotherapy yesterday at 11:30 and felt very depressed about the limited movement in my arm. I cried as they helped me to stretch out my arm and chest muscles that have the nerve and tissue damage from surgery. The nurses gave me some great exercises and sent me on my way. I will do these every day until the movement is back. Feeling determined! I believe the best partnerships happen when we are holding hands and looking forward in the same direction. Speaking of that, Tylen is standing beside Jaden and looking forward with him. He is one of Jaden's good friends. We met Ty and his mom in the boot room of the Elementary School on the first day of kindergarten. Jaden and Ty went happily forward into the new experience while Ty's mom and I cried it out in the boot room as our confident boys marched off for a new adventure. I think they were tears of happiness but I'm not sure. So anyway, Ty is on Jaden's football team and they have remained friends through the years and today when I picked Jaden up from practice, his mom gave me a picture that Ty had drawn for me. I cried and this time I know that it was happy tears.

Unfortunately, my exercise bike seized up so I asked on Facebook if anyone had one they wanted to get rid of. Stacey is bringing one over on Saturday. I love my friends. Love is what keeps us alive. A hug can save a life you know. The best love is the kind that awakens the soul and makes us reach for more. It's the kind that plants a fire in your heart and brings peace to your mind.

Went to Walmart today and got passport pictures taken. The boys and I are making plans to take some trips to the United States in the next few years. We are visualizing Arizona, Florida and maybe Mexico. I've always wanted to go to an all-inclusive resort. The Tulum Ruins are calling me. Today I thought to myself, what if I had the super power to calm my inner storms one breath at a time? Imagine how different my world would be. Then I realized that I do have that super power. ☺

Went for a walk this morning and came home feeling amazing and inspired to write so here you go as I share my writing meditation with you:

<u>From Dark to Light</u>

The stars were still out as I left. The morning air was cool on my face. Step by step around the Deer Meadow track. The sun begins to rise and silhouette the trees against the light. The stars fade. The wind blows the leaves and they rustle and fall from the trees. My shoes crunch on the gravel of the track and I hear a flock of geese flying south for the winter. Can I come too? Not now. I need to be here. Like a treasure being revealed, the sun rises and I see the frost sparkling on the leaves and grass like diamonds. The smell, yes the smell. So fresh and crisp and cool.

I can't wait to email this and share it with Brian. He has been such a wonderful email friend! It's so nice to share my words and inspiration with him.

Journal entry (8th) – It's Thanksgiving weekend and I am thankful for so much! I feel happy. I feel eager anticipation. I feel love. My eyes are viewers and projectors and I am following my internal GPS. Time to stretch, shower, blanket, tea and read then my adorable boys will be awake soon. I love my life. It's going to be a great day.

Confidence - believe in yourself and you'll always be standing on solid ground. This is what I have printed on my business card for teaching. It means so much more now. Today is also a football day. Those football players inspire me. They try so hard and give it all they got. Battered and bruised they just keep on going. Their parents are pretty magnificent too.

Chantal offered to take some family pictures of the boys and me. She's the best. We haven't had any pictures taken for years. We had an awesome day playing in the trees and enjoying the wonderful fall weather. Nature is so healing. Everything is energy and energy is everything. I can't wait to see the pictures. Thank you Chantal! Even though my scars were hidden in the pictures, I know they are there and they remind me of where I have been but they don't dictate where I am going. So I have decided that when I die, I don't want to arrive in a perfectly maintained body. I want to slide in sideways like I used to when I played baseball and there will be dust flying and I will scream, "Wahoo! That was a great trip around the bases. I score!"

October twelfth was a Big appointment day in Calgary. An all-day affair at the hospital. Bone scans, ultrasound on my liver, chest X-rays, bloodwork, EKG's and a visit to the Women's clinic. Phew! I'm feeling very poked and prodded. I'm going home to hug my boys. Everyone sleep tight knowing that your prayers are working.

So blessed to have so many true friends! A true friend knows your weaknesses but focuses on your strengths. They feel your fears but remind you to focus on your faith. They see your anxieties and recognize your disabilities and flaws but go out of their way to emphasize your beauty and your possibilities. Speaking of true friends, I had lunch with my beautiful friend Nancy and then made a trip to Red Deer to pick up a wig. On the way I cranked the tunes and sang at the top of my lungs and felt really good when I arrived at Red Deer. As I stepped out of the car, a bird flew over me and dropped a feather for me. It was so captivating! Yet another example of what is right in what could be a lot of wrong.

Speaking of true friends, Karen and her three amazing kids stopped by earlier this month and dropped off a turkey for the boys and me for Thanksgiving. What a delightful family, what beautiful hearts! Thanks Karen.

This day brought more appointments in the city. I had a mega scan x-ray and met Joan from the Tom Baker Cancer Centre. She is a resource counsellor and will help us financially in every way she can. I'm feeling relieved and grateful. It feels weird asking for help but I guess this is part of the learning. It's okay to accept help if I need it and I could use all the help I can get right now. Speaking of help, I get tears when I write about this one. Dad and Irene have also said that they will help the boys and me while I heal and get back on my feet. Nan also said that she would help us out. It feels good knowing that all I have to focus on now is healing. Hocus, Pocus, Focus. ☺ Feeling blessed that I can take this year off work. My bucket was empty and I got sick. Time to fill it back up again and that is happening with the help and love of so many!

Journal entry (26ᵗʰ) -Bought Jaden a new set of dress up duds from Marks Work Wearhouse. He is being a helper for the Autumn Fundraiser. Neil, Jaden's coach, also told me tonight that Jaden was nominated to be one of the four All-stars from the football team and we will be going to the All-star banquet in Stettler on November eighth. Jaden doesn't know yet. So exciting! Also today, I went to parent/teacher interviews with Zach. So happy that my little man is doing so well in grade three. He said to me, "My job is to do good in school and your job is to get healthy again. I'm doing my part". He is so wise beyond his years. Love my boys and I am so proud of both of them.

I am gathering pledges now for the head shave event at Deer Meadow on November seventh. It feels good to be able to give back. There is football on Saturday and maybe the Pumpkin Hunt with Zach. Then spookiness and fun will be had for Halloween on Monday. Also, next week Jaden gets his Hurtz appliance off his teeth and braces on the bottom. When he is at that orthodontist appointment, I will be taking our passports in to the government office to get Okayed. One more step towards our cool travel plans.

October twenty eighth brought me to Hurdle #1. Bloodwork and then Friday is chemotherapy. Scared but I feel like I am in the right hands with my doctor and like I'm doing the right thing for me right now. I am trusting in my journey. I have a great medical support team as well as a great social support team too. Blessed! I see the goal and I'm enjoying every day. Janet is always texting me to ask me what my number is on a scale of one to ten. What a sweetheart. Today I am a nine.

Reflect - Have you ever felt so depressed that it impacted your physical health and if yes then how did you overcome it?

November - DESPAIR

Well, that chemo #1 hurdle left me flat on my face and crying in the dirt - for a whole week. Yes for truly facing the feeling of despair! I've picked myself up and dusted myself off and now I know what to expect and that yes, as people keep telling me, this too shall pass. Optimism helped me overcome despair this month. Two weeks to focus on feeling good, doing healthy things and loving me and the boys. Drip, drip drip, my bucket is filling back up. Note to self - plan NOTHING for the first week after chemo!

I did make a couple of new friends on chemo day in the hospital and I feel blessed for that. Ella came and talked to me during the five hour infusion session. She's a twenty year survivor of breast cancer and she was also a single mom at the time. She shared her story which gave me a lot of hope and courage. She said she would look for me again on my next chemo day. I hope I see her again. I feel she is one of my earth angels. I also met Michael at the pay booth for parking. He was a really nice guy who sat and talked to me for an hour while I waited for Irene to come and pick me up. He was there visiting a friend. I hope I see him again one day too! Wendy said to me, "You are unreal. Just had chemo and you are flirting with cute guys." Funny sister!

Journal entry (5th) - I went Christmas shopping with some girlfriends. We checked out some of our beautifully decorated small town stores. I am now in the Christmas spirit. The owners put so much love into their businesses and that is what makes them so delicious to shop at. I bought a Believe plaque for my house and a mix to make homemade guacamole. I had to get a ride home early because I started to feel very tired and weak. This evening Janet, Perry and the girls came for a visit. Need sleep now.

Head shave assembly was today at Deer Meadow at nine o'clock. The boys came with me. Good bye my gorgeous long hair. See you in six months. Come back thicker and more beautiful than before. And it was perfect timing because just this morning I brushed my hair and it was starting to fall out in chunks. The head shave event was awesome. I had the whole school giving me support and positive energy and I had my friend Paulette getting her head shaved right beside me! Nancy was in the audience too. I hand in the money tomorrow. I raised about $800 in pledges. I wonder how much the school raised in total? I form partnerships with authentic, surrendered, balanced, healthy, powerful, loving, happy, inspired people because that is what I am. They are a reflection of me. I can always tell when it is a Sunday because I have more energy and I feel better and full of love. I know that there are many friends from many of the different churches around town who pray for the boys and me during their Sunday services. I am convinced this is why I feel so energized today. Janet talked to me on the phone and she said, "Welcome back honey".

On the eighth, went with Jaden and Zach to Stettler for the All-star banquet. It was a great time. Proud momma occasion! It was the first time I wore the wig and probably the last - it was crazy uncomfortable. If my head gets cold this winter I would rather just wear a toque that says "Bulldog Football".

The eleventh was of course Remembrance Day. I was thinking about grandma and grandpa a lot that day because they both made big contributions to peace in World War II, as well as having a big influence on my life. Grandma and I share much in common. They also have a beautiful love story. I remember having sleep overs at their house and to this day I still love the smell of coffee and toast. I don't drink coffee but I love the smell because it reminds me of good times at their house. My sisters and I would sleep in the basement and we were allowed to come upstairs when we smelled the coffee and toast. Every morning grandpa would make grandma breakfast in bed and on those mornings when we stayed, we would come and crawl in bed and talk about what our day would bring. I know they are watching over me from heaven. The boys and I held hands and observed one minute of silence at 11:11:11. Things are lined up just as they need to be!

The thirteenth was a lady friend day with Jan, Char, Lin and Chris. I walked over and hung out at Jan's house and came home with a bunch of beautiful new caps to keep me warm this winter – inside and out. When something unexpected jumps into your life, you can really see the beauty and love that surrounds you. I appreciate so much these days!

Journal entry (14th) - I spent $930 for new tires and a car checkup. Ouch! But at least now I know the boys and I can get where we need to go and Jaden is happy that he won't have to push me out of the alley this winter. ☺ Prevention is Key ☺

Journal entry (15th) - It's a celebration day. Zach is nine today. I am going to volunteer for his first ever day of curling. Then tonight, he gets to open his presents under the Christmas tree, which he helped put up yesterday. He requested bacon and eggs and chocolate cake with ice cream for supper. Sweet nine year old!

There is blood work tomorrow, on the sixteenth, in Olds. A visit with my doctor the next day in Calgary and I am also going shopping for a prosthetic. I heard that Compassionate Beauty is a great place to shop. Then Friday is Hurdle #2. My friend and neighbor, Bob, is going to drive me. I hope I see Ella there. I know what to expect this time and I know in my heart that I am right where I need to be. I CAN DO THIS! Hey, I just noticed that the word CAN is in the word cancer. I told Zach that chemo was going to give me another forty years and Zach said, "Mom, you are going to live to be 111!" Sweet boy. I am so blessed! Note to self - NOTHING is planned for the first week after chemo.

Reflect - When was a time you turned despair into optimism?

17

December - POWERLESSNESS

I made it through chemotherapy hurdle #2 and I have a week left to feel good before the next round. I hung around in powerlessness a lot these past two weeks. Actually any time I wasn't sleeping it was present to some degree. Now that I have experienced feeling crappy, I really see the beauty of the good days. Ella wasn't at the infusion day but the nurses said she would be there for my chemo #3. Even though she wasn't there, I could feel her calm presence as I got my medical treatment.

On November twenty fifth I took the boys to the wave pool in Calgary. They had a great day playing on the waterslides and in the waves. I spent lots of time relaxing in the hot tub. We stopped in Airdrie where we discovered our new favorite restaurant, Swiss Chalet. They both love ribs. I didn't know they could eat that much. I'm sure that the waitress was wondering if I ever feed them at home.

I fought off a cold and I slept lots on the couch the whole weekend after. One time I woke up to this conversation. "Zach do you want a grilled cheese sandwich?" and the reply, "Yes please Jaden. I'm just rubbing mom's feet." Then I drifted off again. I'm so blessed!

Yesterday was Zach's sharing day and I took No-feet, our snake, to the school. Zach was so cute. He is so good at sharing. Speaking of No-feet, I took her out of her cage to get her ready to go to the school and she snuggled in on my scar from the mastectomy and just relaxed there. She is my healing snake. She appreciates the fact that I nursed her back to health when she escaped her cage and spent six months under the stairs. I better also mention Frisco, our kitty. It's amazing the healing power of a purring, snuggling kitty.

I am surrounded by angels that are physical and non-physical. Also yesterday at four o'clock the boys got haircuts at Rundlestone Spa. They look so handsome. I didn't realize how long their hair was getting. It was a much needed cut. I bet people were thinking that I had two girls, not two boys. Jaden has never requested a haircut BUT he did this one. ☺

Today, a BIG Christmas surprise! Deer Meadow chose to help our family instead of doing the usual Christmas gift exchange. Char came over tonight with $1130 in cash and a huge stocking full of presents. Happy tears! It will be a great Christmas. I can go buy the boys anything they want. We chatted about what we would want if we could get something special for Christmas. Zach would like a Connect for X-Box and Minecraft. Jaden would like the new Call of Duty 3 and Assassins Creed. Game Stop, here I come. It's still hard emotionally for me when I think of all the people who are rooting for the boys and me. I have always been very independent and have been able to do everything myself so this was a blow to my EGO and I guess that is a good thing. I told the nurses in the hospital some of my stories and they told me to just say thank you and to let people help us if they chose to because it makes them feel like they are doing something to make my situation better, and they are! I guess that this is all part of the learning journey.

Journal entry (2nd) - This coming weekend brings bowling. Zach goes with Donavan's birthday party Saturday and Jaden goes Sunday with his football wrap up party. Looking forward to a massage with Aly, as a gift from my beautiful friend Nancy, and then to celebrating Christmas with my family on the seventeenth. Also, I'm visualizing a nice skate at Deer Meadow's outdoor rink with Zach during the week that I feel good and of course the thermos of hot chocolate that goes with that.

Zach needs to stay healthy if he wants to come with me on December ninth to the third chemo treatment. You can do it Zach. He has so many questions about what happens to me during a treatment. My little scientist always needs to know more. Jaden has no interest in coming and I'm ok with that. Janet is going to meet us there just in case Zach needs to go for a walk.

He did it, he stayed healthy. Zach came with me for chemo #3 and Janet came too. I drove us down to Calgary and back to Olds, for the treatment. I won't do that again. I'm sure that if I had been pulled over, the officer would have thought I was intoxicated because I wasn't feeling sure of myself on the road. Zach snuggled in the bed with me during the treatment and we watched a show on the TV. He had lots of questions for the nurses and they were very patient and sweet with him. Ella came by and sat with us for a while and her and Zach hit it off. She said that she'll try and be there for the rest of my treatments. Beautiful angel lady! Zach and Janet went for some food and I drifted off for a rest and after that the treatment was over.

I got some love notes from friends and I am feeling grateful today.

- "Carol - I'm so happy to hear you are home and in good spirits. I'm praying for your health and speedy recovery. I ran in the Terry Fox Run in Olds yesterday and thought of you the whole time. Lots of love to you and your family, Dawn"
- "Carol - You are an inspiration to all of us... thank you for your strength, courage, warmth and compassion! The juice, nuts, muffins are our 'healthy fix' for those days you know you need to eat, but the chemo has other plans. Nuts, dark fruits, dried fruits = strength. The frozen 'stuff' is for the boys on the days where they are hungry but no one is motivated or prepared to cook. I know your spirit is full... we will help with your stomachs. Jamie-Dee and Mike"
- "Carol - Keep your thoughts positive and optimistic and see yourself as healthy and whole. Your positive energy, thoughts, visualizations, affirmations, prayer and meditation combined with whatever medical treatment you choose to seek will serve to enhance your healing process. Jan"

Journal entry (12th) - I'm thinking of my Deer Meadow School Family, my Bulldog Football Family, my Facebook Family and my Olds Community Family. So many friends helped us and I'm sure I am forgetting some and I am sorry for that. I blame chemo-brain, which by the way is a real thing. I have to make lists for everything or I forget and more than once I went downstairs and when I got there I had forgotten why I went. I am praying that this goes away after the treatments along with all the other nasty side effects. I'm sure it will.

December thirtieth brings Chemo #4 and I made a Facebook post that expresses the fact that I am – enjoying the day and thinking that 2011 was a huge year of growth for the boys and I and we are looking forward to all the cool doors that are going to open for us in 2012. I said that it's going to be a great year - I feel that in my heart. We are wishing a Happy New Year to our fabulous family and friends. We have appreciated the love and support in 2011 and look forward to living, loving and laughing with everyone next year. I didn't post that two chemo treatments in one month made for a hard month. I look forward to future, healthier Christmas breaks. I want everyone to see my optimistic side so I don't scare or worry anyone. I was definitely feeling quite powerless this month. On a good note, Irene drove me for chemo #4 and Ella was there for a hug.

Reflect - Can you think of a time that you felt powerless and how did you overcome it?

January - INSECURITY

I slept a lot in the last two weeks. I was lucky to be able to get the boys off to school each morning then to be able to sleep all day so that I would have the energy to make supper and do homework with the boys. On the weekends the boys fended for themselves quite a bit as I slept on the couch. My appetite was way down and I lost weight because nothing tasted good. My mouth and throat and eyes had sores on them and it hurt to swallow. I ached all over and spent a lot of time in the bathtub soaking in Epsom salts. I'm feeling good today and releasing insecurity about the future. I have a positive attitude and I am living in the moment. My insecurity about tomorrow has eased and I am just going with the flow. What is going to happen will happen whether I worry about it or not and actually if I worry about it then it is more likely to happen because that is where I am focussing my energy.

So, it's week three of Chemo #4 with two hurdles left. I see and feel the light at the end of the tunnel. The symptoms are less scary now because I know what to expect. The 'tired' feeling is building and I look forward to being 100% here for the boys very soon. They say that we get more resilient in tough situations so I conclude that I have raised two boys who are very resilient. I'm also looking forward to getting back to work too, I would rather be there than here. I miss my Deer Meadow family. Love and Light, (((Hugs))) and Smiles ☺

On the fourteenth Zach and I went and bought three new snails for our fish tank and Zach named them Hope, Believe and Miracle. The next day it was very cold and we truly appreciated the warmth and love in our home as we watched our new snails settle into their new home.

Hurdle #5 is done. Irene drove me and Ella came and sat with me. Here are three comments from Facebook because I need to sleep.

- From Brian – "Just remember the sun is always shining behind the clouds."
- From Jody – "Hurdle 5 down!! Your positivity and focus on potential is inspiring! Your upcoming trips sound exciting for you and the boys."
- From Abby – "Ms. Taylor I just wanted to tell you, you inspire me in so many ways, I hope when I am older I will find people with hearts as golden as yours. Thank you."

Reflect - Was there ever a time when you released insecurity and fear and surrendered to what was?

February - GUILT

Feeling some guilt today, as if I may have compromised my standards and violated my body. Feeling weak and I need to remind myself to trust and breathe. My emotions are all over the place these days. I'm on a rollercoaster ride of emotions big time but I know in my heart that if I focus on integrity and doing what is right for me then there will be less guilt.

Got a burst of energy today and got lots done. Yes, to feeling good. Only one treatment left. Let the celebrating begin. I'm visualizing our trip to Phoenix in May. Deep breath... Sigh. I LOVE my family and friends. Looking forward to going to the Elementary School family dance with Zach tonight!

I did it! I'm done hurdle #6 and just getting over the side effects. Irene drove me and I saw my angel friend Ella and she said she would phone and check up on me. It's time to focus on what I want - Abundance in all areas of my life. Hey - I have that right now. Life is good. I love me. All good things flow to me. Note to self – declutter and get rid of what does not serve you, forgive, follow your heart and always remember to find balance. Immerse yourself in life, see the sacredness. Try not to think too much. Just be aware and look and listen and feel.

I have goose bumps and a lump in my throat. Guess what was delivered to my house. We just received flowers, a card and money from some 'mystery friends'. That just made my day. There is so much rightness in my world. I can't wait to tell the boys!

Darrell stopped by on the twentieth to drop off the child support payment. He seemed different, calmer. He looked me straight in the eye and told me to be strong. Reflecting back on my failed marriage, I see that my bucket was empty for the last three years of our marriage. It's no wonder everything fell apart. I would have left me too. I will always consider Darrell a soulmate. To me, a soulmate helps you learn more about yourself and he definitely did that. Thanks Darrell. I forgive me and I forgive you. I am also very appreciative to Darrell's girlfriend because without her the separation of Darrell and I would have taken a lot longer than it did. Darrell and I needed to separate so that we could each grow more.

Reflect - Think of a situation when you used integrity to do the right thing so that you would have less guilt.

March - UNWORTHINESS

I dedicated time this month to learning more about meditation. I feel my strength slowly returning. Caring for myself and learning about new things has helped me move through some feelings of unworthiness. When my mind grows quiet and still then I can face self-defeating thought patterns and gently release them so that more space opens up for positive thoughts to flow in. So I learned that for me, doing anything in a mindful way is a meditation. With that being said, I did a shoveling meditation.

There was a big dump of snow and the boys and I went out to shovel. It was so much fun as we worked together one shovelful at a time. We laughed and threw snowballs and just kept on working to get through it all. Then we stood back and admired our work. We are powerful when we work together. After all the work was done and hot chocolate was being consumed, of course with extra mini marshmallows, I stood by the window and looked outside for some time. It was snowing again and it looked so beautiful. Just like a snow globe. I dressed up and went outside and marveled at the beauty. The flakes were slowly floating down to land where they were destined to be and it was so calm and peaceful. The streetlights glinted off the newly fallen snow and made them look like diamonds. Zach banged on the window and smiled and waved and made a heart shape with his hands. I made a heart shape back and I looked around my yard and thought to myself, I am very rich!

Went for bloodwork and a visit with my doctor. He said all looks good but he wants me to put some weight back on. I lost forty pounds in six months. That shouldn't be a problem now that food tastes so good again. I did some long, hard thinking, feeling and praying to answer the question, "Do I need to take the Tomoxafin?" The answer keeps coming back as "no". I need to focus on healing and being healthy now. My body can't handle any more medical stuff if I want to get strong again. AND I DO! I'm listening to my heart on this. I have made a choice and I will live with it. I will not be a "sheeple". I am abundant in all areas of my life. I posted on Facebook, "HAPPY! HAPPY! HAPPY! The doctor gave me a clean bill of health. The boys and I are celebrating every day. What a learning experience this has been. Let the good times roll! Have an awesome day.... we will! Thank you again for being there for us - wonderful family and friends." This post got forty likes and forty-one comments. Here are a few of the comments. I enjoyed reading them so much that I wanted to share the joy.

- Joanne said," Awesome! Your positivity & grace throughout are an inspiration."
- Talva said, "Carol. This is fabulous news. Sending love and hugs... I am very excited and will be calling dad soon to share this great news!"
- Jamie-Dee said, "Yeah!!! Big cheers can be heard from the Marshall house."
- Chantal said, "Awesome news Carol! I know you'll be able to inspire others to fight it as well! Huge hug!"
- Alicia said, "Oh Carol what fabulous news.....so happy for you (and your boys!) Enjoy every day!!!!"
- Janet said, "You are an inspiration to all of us big sister .... there was never a doubt in my mind that you would totally kick this thing but so glad that the treatments are over and that you and the boys get your life back. Your strength and grace through the experience will remain with me forever. Xoxoxo"
- Joanne said, "Awesome. I can't wait to see who you become; optimistic and improved. Look out world!"

It's finally spring and it feels extra special this year. The new growth and the new baby calves in the field. The sun feels amazing and warm on my face. All feels so fresh and clean and new. It's like I'm seeing spring through all new eyes. It's hard to explain. I just got back from skating with Zach and his school class. They are so adorable. On the way to my car I found a penny lying on the ground. For me this signifies abundance.

Reflect - There are many ways to meditate. What works for you to bring you right to this present moment? Right here – Right now.

April - JEALOUSLY

I worked through some negative thoughts, jealousy and insecurities about my physical appearance this month. I'm now comfortable with my bald head and peach fuzz. I have some new goals and a burning desire to achieve them. I have already stated my wishes and they are coming to me as soon as I prove that I can focus and achieve my main goal – improved health. It is all there in the unknown and it's waiting for and will flow to me. A lot of it is off my radar but it's going to be more than I wished for. I'm lucky because I get to live the rest of my life in the flow. What a gift. I am happiest when I'm in the process of achieving my goals. I follow my bliss. I live an extraordinary life. With that being said, I'm looking forward to going to Red Deer to see the *Hunger Games* movie with the boys. We also want to go and have fun at the wave pool in Calgary. I discovered that peace does not mean to be in a place where there is no noise, trouble or hard work. It means to be in the midst of those things and still be calm in your heart and I am feeling calm in my heart. Speaking of calm and peaceful, my calm and peaceful boy turns fifteen this month. I am so lucky to have him in my life. He is amazing and he makes me so proud every day. I look forward to going to the farm with the boys to play soon.

Zach and I went to the playground and were playing on the equipment. I told him about the old merry-go-rounds that we used to have when I was a little girl. We would get them going so fast that we could hang on to the bars and the centrifugal force would allow our legs to fly out from under us and we would be hanging from our arms. If we got going too fast then we would be flung off and end up in a pile bruised and battered. When I got home, I thought about this some more. Life is kind of like a merry-go-round. If you get going too fast then you get flung off. A good reason to slow down today, breathe and be balanced. Also, always remember that life is a playground. Have fun! On the way home we spent some time driving and listening to music. It was very healing. Our favorite songs were "Firework" by Katy Perry and "Unwritten" by Natasha Bedingfield. Check out the lyrics on YouTube.

We can choose to have a pity party and make ourselves and those around us sad and miserable or we can choose to have a happy party so that we and those around us feel strong and confident. The choice is up to each of us and the amount of work is the same. Today I tune myself to the frequency of happy, strong and confident.

Reflect – Have you ever been flung off in the bushes? How did you recover?

May - HATRED

Hate, like all emotions, is natural. We are blessed to be able to feel all our emotions. When we feel hate, we send out a huge rocket of desire to change because it feels so bad in the body. I discovered that peace and love feel so much better than hatred.

May third came and went and what a wonderful birthday I had. I think that it's so important to celebrate all these milestones because things can change in the blink of an eye. This month I lost my hatred of cancer by feeling what hate feels like in my body then shifting my thoughts so that I now appreciate the experience because it has taught me so much. Acceptance and letting go of the resistance feels so much better! I am so blessed and grateful. I worked at Deer Meadow School surrounded by friends, got loads of Facebook greetings, supper at the Flames with the boys and then the *Chipwrecked* movie at the Elementary School. I'm gonna have sweet dreams tonight. This is going to be my best year yet!

Trip to Arizona

Right Here – Right Now. And away we go! Arizona here we come. One of our visualizations is coming true. Friday we left home and slept at Janet and Perry's from 11:00 pm to 2:45 am. We took a taxi to the airport and had a nice flight from Calgary to Denver. Lunch at the airport and then caught the flight from Denver to Phoenix. Thank goodness that Zach was such a good co-pilot. ☺ The stewardess saw Zach's enthusiasm on the plane and asked him if he would like to sit in the cockpit with the pilot after we landed.

Of course he said yes and the cool thing was that he said to me, that he was going to sit in the cockpit and I said, "Good luck with that" and sure enough he did. He is such a great manifester. I need to take lessons. So next we all piled into the minivan and headed to the condo. The plants are so cool and different here. Drove along and just took in the beauty of it all. The condo is an awesome place and Jen, Janet and Perry's friend, made an amazing cake and left it at the condo for us upon our arrival. We unpacked and settled in then went shopping for food. On the way back, we stopped and had the best ribs ever at Shane's Ribs. Jaden said they were even better than Swiss Chalet. Went back to the condo and unpacked the groceries and then went and had a swim in the pool. Extremely tired tonight.

I slept in late and Zach slept for thirteen hours. A little jet lag, I believe. It's Mother's Day today. I am so blessed to be the mother of these two amazing boys. Janet's husband Perry took us all out for lunch and we wandered through the cool shops at Westgate. Jaden bought a Patriots hat and Zach chose a Patriots freezer cup as a souvenir. Super-hot, like forty degrees Celsius. The boys and I have never experienced this kind of heat. They have water misting out of restaurants and stores. It's so refreshing. Came back after shopping and had a nice cool swim. We went to the exercise room then back to the pool. I found a penny when I was walking and I took lots of pictures today. I love the plants that grow around here. Tonight, Janet and Perry went to the LA vs Coyotes game and I was the lucky auntie who got to tuck in my beautiful nieces, Maddy and Mia. LA won four to two. You win some and you lose some. As long as you learn a lesson then it isn't a loss. A fun day.

It's Monday today. We hung around the pool and workout room all day. Ahhh... this is the life! I so needed to just relax and let it all go. Travelling is fun like that. It shows us all kinds of new things and forces us to be totally present in the moment.

The day was relaxed and comfortable. We spent quiet time on the deck admiring the baby birds that were in the nest on the ledge. They were so sweet and little and waited so eagerly for their parents to return with food for them. They were just so innocent and surrendered to life and all that was happening. They brought peace to me, just by watching them. Nature is powerful! The evening was exhilarating and fast moving. We went to the Coyotes vs Kings game and it was awesome fun. The floating taco made Zach's day. We saw Auntie Misti, Jeff and Grandma Irene. Grandma gave the boys some money to buy special souvenir t-shirts. Zach chose a burgundy one and Jaden chose a white one. The Coyotes lost four to nothing but it was still awesome fun. I was feeling chilled in the stands at the ice rink, it felt real cold compared to the outside air, and was snuggled up in my seat to keep warm. Knees tucked in. I was sitting beside the stairs and a nice girl smiled at me and said, "You look cold" and I said, "Yes, a little." On her way back down the stairs she gave me her sweater and said, "Keep it!" I gave her a hug and she was on her way. What an amazing act of kindness. There are so many wonderful people in this world!

When we got back to the condo, we went for a night swim and then ate cheese cake. YUM! Zach and I are just writing in our journals then it's sweet dreams for us. I explained to Zach that journaling is a great way to unleash your true feelings. It is a powerful and therapeutic activity and it's very much like having a conversation with yourself. This writing we will keep but I also told him that it is good sometimes to write an angry letter then to throw it away as you throw away the negative feelings. I told him that when I write I don't think about what I'm writing. I just let it flow. There is no editing, questioning or judging, just free and beautiful writing as the words just flow onto the paper. He gets it because this flow happens to him too.

Perry flew out to Vegas today for his pool tournament. Janet and the kids and I got the truck fixed then went to a burger place. When we got back we worked out in the gym then splashed in the pool. Loving Life! Tomorrow we get to meet Jen and Ethan, new friends and new connections. We really are all one. Tomorrow we leave to go to Vegas baby!

A beautiful five hour drive with so many tumbleweeds and cactus. Getting there was half the fun. We stopped and checked out Hoover Dam and took some nice pictures there. It felt so humid and fresh at the Dam compared to the dry, wide open desert. Such contrast! Life is awesome like that. We stayed at Circus Circus. What a cool hotel. There is a swimming pool, a circus and an amusement park right in the hotel. We drove the strip and went to Old Vegas. People were dressed up in interesting costumes and others were zip lining down the main street. I think I want to zip line one day. Yes, I will make that happen. There is sooooo much to see. There are so many beautiful lights. We were told that the astronauts on the International Space Station can see Vegas from space. I totally believe that! Went to the Adventure Dome theme park then went for a swim at the pool. Had a delicious buffet and went back for a second time to the Adventure Dome. A busy day and everything just felt so right.

Checked out at Vegas then we headed to Page, Arizona. It was a delightful drive with lots of red rocks. Supper and then the kids had a swim at the hotel. We have crazy Canadian kids, swimming in an unheated pool. We made the owners and the local people smile. We grow them tough in Canada. ☺ It was an early bed after a long day of travelling.

The next day, we toured Antelope Canyon. WOW! Just WOW! The tour guide took some amazing pictures for me with my camera. He knew just where to stand with the light to get the best pictures so I was more than happy to give him my camera. I can't wait to see the pictures bigger and more beautiful when I put them on my computer. I think I'll make a video for Janet and Perry and one for us as well. There is such a history to this place. Antelope Canyon was formed by erosion of Navajo sandstone and is primarily due to flash flooding. Rainwater runs into the basin above the slot canyon sections, picking up speed and sand as it rushes into the narrow passageways. Over time the passageways eroded away, making the corridors deeper and smoothing hard edges in such a way as to form characteristic flowing shapes in the rock. Go to google images to see the beauty that I am talking about!

We drove south to Horseshoe canyon and Perry and the kids and I went for a hike. It was very hot and we drank lots of water but it was so worth it to see the view. South again and stopped in Jerome, a little town that was nestled in the hills, and had ice cream and then moved on south some more. Next stop the Grand Canyon! It was a little foggy when we were there but the kids really enjoyed walking around and stretching their legs. Then south some more and we checked into the house in Sedona. An appealing old house with lots of character and the crazy Canadian kids swam in the unheated pool again. Busy, awesome day!

It's Perry's birthday today. We hiked Bell Rock and Janet found me a heart shaped red rock. It's going home as my souvenir and it will find a permanent spot on my bedside table with my other rocks and gems. Hearts are special to me and a heart shaped red rock from Sedona that was given to me by my classy siStar is extra special! It even smells like Sedona. I took some amazing pictures of the boys with Bell Rock in the background. The kids wanted to climb and climb all day long up that enticing rock but Perry and I got tired and made the executive decision to head down. If only I could bottle the energy of kids, I would be rich! We saw some cool and twisted trees. The force is strong here. ☺ Next, we went for some water fun to cool off at a place called Rock Slide Park. It was a natural waterslide right in the rocks. It was such an unreal magnificent place. I could feel the energy of the vortexes. There were huge butterflies drinking from puddles and my time here stood still. A little piece of heaven on earth. Good memories are being had here. We walked around a little novelty store and found all kinds of cool things to look at. We all enjoyed the place except Jaden. Browsing stores is not something he likes to do. We had supper at the pub and then went back to the house, where the kids swam in the unheated pool with candles flickering all around. There wasn't a light in the backyard so the kids had a fun candle light swim. Janet and Perry went out for Perry's birthday then returned in time to have carrot cake before bed. A sweet day!

A picture in the hallway of the house has marvelous words and I stopped to really read what it was saying. I felt warm and light as I walked to the bathroom where there on the wall was another poem that had the same kind of message but different words. Both of them gave me a similar feeling and that was to look inside myself with love and trust. I feel so inspired. The sun warms my face and my soul here. I will be back!

The next day we travelled back to Phoenix and went to Sunsplash Water Park. Had a blast! Zach said it was the best day yet. For me, it's hard to compare because every day was beautiful in its own way. We had supper at the Island Restaurant then relaxed in the hot tub. I'm going to head to the swimming pool and exercise room when I get done writing this, so that I can go and get some exercise and some innercise. I love spending time relaxing by the pool with the boys and with my family. We leave tomorrow. I had a blast but I look forward to being home to see Frisco and No feet. Ever grateful for the Arizona experience. Memories, memories, memories! I love you Janet, Perry, Maddy and Mia. Thanks so much for sharing that memory with us and for making this trip possible.

The beauty of this trip has inspired me to write today. I love it when I get in that flowy writing mood. I wake up in the middle of the night with a burning desire to write something down. I keep paper and pen by my bed. It's like spirit is flowing through me and I just write and write and write and time just stands still.

On the trip back home, I noticed that the stewardess said to us on take-off that if there is an emergency situation that we should put the oxygen on ourselves first. This caught my attention because in my mind, I would help my kids get the oxygen first. I thought about this for quite a while and decided that they were indeed right! If I don't take care of myself first then I am no good to my kids or anyone else. It's okay for me to look after myself and it's not selfish, it is a necessity!

I think that acceptance is seeing with your heart, not with your eyes and that attitude is a little thing that makes a BIG difference. I have a healing attitude and use the power of visualization, the magic of my imagination, the healing properties of laughter, the miracle of changing perception and this will help me find the meaning behind my illness. The cause and prevention. I am moving from illness to wellness, from I to WE. I ask myself... What do I want... what do I want that is new? What do I want to let go? And what do I want to stay the same? I am listening to my body's wisdom. I am embracing silence. I don't judge others. I eliminate toxins that are emotional and physical. I relinquish my need for approval. I relinquish my hatred and opposition. I live in the present moment and I replace FEAR with LOVE.

Reflect – Have you ever been like an alchemist who transmuted hate to love?

June - REVENGE

I think that the best revenge is to focus on all the beauty that surrounds me and achieve massive success that way. Yes to Success!

Hanging with the boys this morning, I took a deep breath and said, "I wonder why this moment feels so perfect?" Zach replied, "Because it is," and Jaden smiled. They help me every day to see the rightness in everything!

According to Wikipedia – Revenge is also called payback and I payback with hugs. Zach is my huggy bear and he picked me the first rose from our yard and Jaden got his first summer job. It's a wonderful day of firsts. I wonder what else will unfold.... excited to find out.

Speaking of hugging, who needs a hug? Hugging is good medicine. It transfers energy and gives the person an emotional lift. I read somewhere that you need four hugs a day for survival, eight for maintenance, and twelve for growth. I feel that hugging is a form of communication because it can say things you don't have the words for. And the nicest thing about a hug is that you usually can't give one without getting one. Love yourself and others unconditionally and be yourself fearlessly. Love combined with Trust = Miracles.

Journal entry (28th) – It has been a busy month as school wraps up and I didn't get a lot of time to journal this month. Time and change just keeps happening. Last day of school and I'm so proud of the way the boys so gracefully moved through this year of challenges, learning and growth. Bring on the fun of summer and some down time!

Reflect - Recall a time that you turned revenge into success.

July - ANGER

Jury is here and so are summer bonfires. I spent some time staring at the coals and embers of our outdoor fire and thought to myself that the coals represent anger for me. If I was to grab a coal with the intent of angrily throwing it at someone or something, it would do the most damage to me. This month I just feel the heat (anger) of that coal but I don't pick it up. I just let it be and enjoy its beauty. I burnt myself a few times during the divorce until it hurt so much that I was finally forced to let it go. I was also angry at myself for getting sick then I realized that my anger was helping to cause it and even actually make it worse. Just let it go or better yet just acknowledge it from a distance and feel its heat but make a wise choice and don't pick it up. I guess if you want then go ahead. It's your choice.

Summer fun! It is wonderful to experience the joy, anticipation and excitement, through Zach, as he prepares himself for the birthday party/camping sleepover that he will be attending with his friends tonight. As Zach puts it and I agree...."Friends are so awesome!"

There was a storm today with lots of lightning and thunder and big rolling clouds. I felt an eerie calm, just before it came, and standing on the back deck I couldn't hear any birds so that freaked me out a little. When the storm hit and I went inside for shelter, I could feel the hair on my neck standing up. It seemed very ominous but then it passed. After the storm had run its course, Zach and I stood outside as a small sprinkle splashed our faces and we marveled at the beauty of the rainbow. We also decided to walk barefoot in the gutter to have some fun. I wonder if our neighbors thought we were crazy. Storms release their anger then move on to better things and it's okay if I do too!

The boys and I went on a road trip. Zach has always wanted to go see a glacier and I am now well enough to take him. The windows are open and the tunes cranked as we sing along to the songs on the radio and drive towards the statuesque mountains. The sun is shining and everything smells so fresh. What a fun adventure! We made it to the mountains and the Athabasca glacier. Yes... STUNNING! We boarded a big bus with tracks and headed up the road with our group. Lots of sharp turns and steep hills but it was a fun ride. We drove out onto the glacier and marveled at how cold it was as we stood on the ice. Just fifteen minutes before we were super-hot in our shorts and t-shirts and now we all wished that we had jackets. Contrast. ☺ Zach was so excited to finally have his wish come true. Before we left, we filled our water bottles and drank a bunch of the fresh, cold glacier mountain water then we filled them back up again. We drank the water and ate snacks all the way back to our hotel in Rocky Mountain House. I feel so amazing - better than I have felt in a long time. Is it the water?

Zach comes running up to me jumping up and down and yelling, "Mom! Mom! He's here! He's here." I thought maybe from his excitement that he had seen an angel. To him it was an angel... an angel on wheels. The ice cream truck is the best on a hot summer day!

Journal entry (24th) - Happy 90th Nan. You have been an amazing great grandma to the boys and an influential special grandma to me. You have inspired me to keep moving forward. So today we celebrated a very special lady on her birthday. She has been a big part of my life for the last twenty six years. We meet people for a reason and I'm glad we met her. She said to me that once we lose our fear of death then we lose all other fears too. This is so true for me because the other day I was climbing up a ladder and realized that my knees weren't shaking. So very cool!

It's just one of those days that you have to go running through the water sprayer and have a water gun fight. We played in our sand box and buried our feet in the sand. I felt so grounded and connected to mother earth. It's so important to remember to just play sometimes. Did you know that the right to play is part of the universal declaration of human rights?

Reflect - Was there ever a time when your anger did more damage to you then it did to the person you were angry at?

August - DISCOURAGEMENT

This month I touched on discouragement briefly but didn't stay there long. Just like anger and the hot coal I have learned to let it go. I focus on being creative. So for me, I will go on with my inspired soul writing.

Summer is for making memories and reenergizing. First, at Calaway Park in Calgary, on the roller coaster sitting up front, arms in the air and enjoying the ride. When we were waiting our turn to ride they had to stop and clean up. Someone didn't find the ride to be as much fun as we do. Second, with cool evenings, those are the best for making chocolate chip cookies. Also, no summer is complete without some hiking in Kananaskis Country with the boys. Our mountains and rivers are so alluring. We drank some water straight from the source and it was pure and wonderful. My bucket is full!

On the ninth we went to Drumheller and played in the badlands. Saw an eagle when we were at the hoodoos and I stopped in my tracks and stared at it, as it was flying so free in the sky. I also found a feather. As the boys climbed all the way to the top, I rested in the shade and smiled as their strong, young bodies explored the hills. At our second stop, it was so intriguing to see the suspension bridge and watch how many people trusted their legs as they walked. It was entertaining to watch the people as they crossed the bridge. Some would cling to the edge and have a total look of terror in their eyes and then there, were my boys. They wait for everyone to get off so they can make it swing back and forth. It's funny how different people react so differently to the same situation. That is something to think about.

I'm just relaxing in my hammock and enjoying my delightful backyard. The boys are in the house, tummies are full after our nice lunch and they are busy doing their own thing. I'm reading books and drinking tea and enjoying the mesmeric, sunny day and now I need to write. It's the flowy feeling.

When you lose your fear of death then all other fears fall away. Things are in alignment for me. The clock said 3:33 and I found a feather which represents freedom for me. I also found a penny the other day on my walk and I'm seeing hearts everywhere. I sliced open a watermelon the other day and it was heart shaped. Cleaned the kitty litter box and found a heart shaped urine clump. Yucky but still cool! I am loved and there are so many physical and non-physical angels around me. Zach and I watched the *Star Wars* movie last week. The FORCE is strong with us. Now that we have conquered the enemy within, no external force can harm us. Our force is within.

I just looked at the garden hose and thought to myself, "If your life is not flowing you just have to stop stepping on the hose." Use Patience, Faith, Forgiveness, Willpower and Acceptance.

I listen to the voices in my head and get rid of discouragement and negativity. I do things to help me grow and I free my mind. I develop a still and alert attention and I focus on my breathing. I let thoughts and feelings be. And right now I am thinking, "Be you and say I love you often. Don't take crap and learn to say no. It's okay to get angry then let it go. I don't obsess about beauty and I take care of my body. I prioritize and live like I mean it and yes, I do take some risks because that is how I grow. Change is growth and growth is the essence to life." It was Wayne Dyer who said that EGO is just Edging God Out. I love that. I release my EGO today. When I was sick I was forced to confront my EGO and grow. I released a lot of resistance. I set big goals and I go for it! Well that was nice to just write. I do hear Zach calling me. I think I hear something about homemade ice tea with mint leaves. Life is great!

Journal entry (18th) - It's a beautiful morning. I'm looking forward to a day of family. Our small town is so fun. There is a parade, a pool party and the *Lorax* movie in the park. I love lying out under the stars and pondering the vastness of our universe!

Good morning – YAWN - Football practice at six in the morning for Jaden. Let the season begin. I admire his dedication, determination and his individual effort to make the season the best it can be for himself and his team. I'm behind you all the way Jaden.

I did it! I got my tattoo. It's amazing and they did such an awesome job. For me, the red heart represents Love and Trust and the pink rose that is wrapped around the heart represents Growth and Beauty. It has two pedals for two boys. The butterfly represents Freedom and the colors on its wings transition from blue to purple to red. Blue for Zach, purple for me and red for Jaden. The heart shows the inner peace and strength that I feel. It shows intuition, emotion, transition and relationships. The rose is single and thorn less and represents admiration, gentleness, gracefulness, appreciation, joy, sweetness, success and strength. The butterfly is a sign of transition, celebration, lightness, soul, faith and change. And mine is a morph butterfly so it's even more beautiful. And beauty, by the way, is in the eye of the beholder. For me, getting this tattoo was something that I had always wanted to do but was afraid to do. I have thought for many days and put a lot of consideration into what it would look like. This is a manifestation of years of thought so it's especially important to me. I Love, Love, Love it. Feeling appreciation for my tattoo artist who is full of creativity!

Reflect - What do you do to express your creativity?

September - BLAME

Blame, yes, Blame. I discovered this month that in the past I may have spent too much time finding other people to blame and too much energy finding reasons and excuses for not being what I was capable of being. So this month I choose to put time and energy into me so that I can grow out of the past and get on with my life. Yes, it is all about letting go of resistance.

Hello my excellent life. I have come a long way in the last six months. I have been busy healing and gaining strength, inside and out. In July, I decided to sign up for a Fitness/Wellness retreat put on by my friend Jamie-Dee and since then I have been manifesting lots of cool things. My sister Wendy is coming with me. I won a $50 gift card for Solara Spa so I booked a detoxifying seaweed wrap. I have been communicating with my friend Ralph who was one of my first friends when I was four or five. The boys are awesome, as always, and all is well in my world. I need to write one more thing that I am very proud of. I have worked my body up to the point where this morning I walked/ran five km, in under an hour. I'm going to keep working on this every day so that I can blast through it on Sept. 30th at the Run for the Cure in Canmore. I love my life. I feel great! Also, a pretty and awe-inspiring sunset tonight. It is in the little things that I see so much rightness. Sweet Dreams!

Looking forward to doing the Terry Fox walk/run with Zach at the Elementary School today and then to getting away to the mountains this weekend to do some hiking and yoga with some wonderful women. Watch out, it's also a full moon!

Oh ya! I did the five km, Run for the Cure, in the mountains with beautiful women. The majestic mountains wrapped me in a cocoon of protection. The air was so fresh and the sights inspired me to run the whole course. I ran the five km slowly, but I still did it. I couldn't keep up with the crowd that was running so I let myself fall back so that I would have enough strength to finish. I looked up and saw Donna jogging on the spot and waiting for me to catch up. She finished the run with me. Super sweet friend!

Home Sweet Home! I'm happy to be home with the boys again. All is good except my extremely sore muscles. I feel like I was run over by the exercise truck. ☺ Epsom salt bath will feel good tonight.

Reflect - Think of a time that you released some resistance from your past and it felt so good that you walked away with a smile on your face? Think of that time now and Smile. ☺

October - WORRY

To all my lady friends. I got my yearly mammogram done this month and all is well. Remember to go get squeezed if you haven't in a while. Worry is exhausting to the body, mind and spirit. Prevention is the key. This month, I also discovered tapping, which is also called EFT. This is a wonderful way to release worry. Check it out on YouTube.

Lucky me, I get to go back to Canmore again this weekend but this time it's Jaden who is going to be doing the sweating, not me. Zach and I are going to hike and watch the game. Go Spartans! Hiking reminds me of all the shades of green there are. One time, at school, we had a color week and all the kids wore green on one of the days. I was shocked at how many shades of green there are out there. Just like people, we are all different, yet all the same!

Journal entry (8th) - Turkey buns and an extra day at home with the boys. Thankful. Thankful. Thankful. Happy Thanksgiving!

What doesn't kill you makes you stronger. Pulled ligaments and torn muscles, keep practicing with those crutches Jaden since you'll need them for hopefully no more than a couple weeks. When I got him off the bus and helped him to the car, I felt his pain. And the Emergency Ward on a Saturday night with two kids is quite a learning experience too. Who knew that this place would be so full of drunk, talkative people who had all sorts of problems and stories to tell?

I was doing some thinking about the past and I thought back to the day that I had my last visit with my divorce lawyer, Brian. He was such a good lawyer and he made the whole process so much easier. Some people say that lawyers are crooks and leeches and stuff like that, but not Brian. He really cared about his job and about me. I walked away from one lawyer who only cared about himself and glad I did. Anyway, on my last visit with Brian we discussed the fact that It was all done. I was ready to go out there and be my true authentic self. I decided to go straight home and eat an orange in a meditative way with my boys. I gave him a hug and was on my way as a Single Mom. I haven't talked to him since. I went home that night and did some journaling about how I was feeling. I came across that writing tonight and it means even more now than it did when I wrote it, so I'm going to write it out again for you.

Brian inspired me to write about being authentic, so here it goes...

I like the number three, so I'm going to write my three steps which I will work on to become more authentic.

1) I will awaken to my authentic self - I will use engaged inquiry practices and I will listen to the answers. Things like meditating, breathing, silence, Pilates and the sway test that Irene taught me. I will ask and then I will listen for the answers.

2) I will align with my authentic self - I will be aware of the choices I am making and the results that I am getting. I will look at my values and see if I'm aligned with them. I value love, trust, growth, beauty and freedom. I will face my negative and limiting beliefs and release them.

3) I will create - I will look for the oneness in everything and I will use my energies to create good things in my life. I will create wonderful relationships, financial success and I will surround myself with all things that make me feel good. I will write, and sing and dance and play and I will enjoy something beautiful about every day.

Hey, that rhymes, cool! Maybe I'll write a kids book some day and that sentence can be in it. I love it when the words flow through me like that!

Reflect - What techniques do you use to release worry?

November - DOUBT

Some of my journal entries may seem inappropriate to others but I give up my doubt and keep on writing. I figure that if you like how I write then you will read on and if you don't then you wouldn't of made it this far. ☺ Doubting is a waste of time for me now because life is too short and too special for it. Zach also harboured no doubt as he did his part in the Remembrance Day performance at the Olds Elementary School. Confidence is key. Proud of you Zach as you show me every day how to live fearlessly and with style. Standing tall and confident and speaking out with clarity and hope. Serious yet smiling as you exude complete balance and harmony in life.

I've been craving more laughter in my life so I'm reading a new book called, *"Laughter is the Breast Medicine (An inspirational book of humor)"* by Eileen Kaplan. It's really funny. It is exactly what I needed today. Laughter is so healing. Speaking of laughter, Jaden is pretty darn funny sometimes too. He'll say something out of the blue and I'll say, "what?" and he will repeat it. Then I crack up. Mr. Witty. He gets that from my Dad. Dad also has that witty sense of humor. Anyway, so now that I'm looking for laughter, I am finding it everywhere. I am such a good creator. I found a crossword puzzle that I had given one of my classes at school about human reproduction during our sex ed. class. The kids needed to work with partners to find all the words in the puzzle and it was a race to see which group of two would get it done first. They were so serious and focused but I couldn't help but to giggle and write down on the back of a copy of the puzzle, some of the things I was hearing from the kids in the class and all in a serious tone of the competition to get it done. Here is just a sample of what I heard. "I'm looking for maturity." and the reply, "I'll let you know when I find it." I laughed so hard when I got home and reread the words. And by the way, all the kids were winners in the end, treats all around. Now that is teaching at its finest. ☺

Our school is the best. We are on the leading edge of education and so much has changed over the last twenty years and I'm happy to be a part of all the positive changes.

I did a stick project one year with my grade seven class. The students brought a special stick from home and I contributed the yarn, paper and some other crafting supplies. This was a combined Art and Language Arts project. The students chose contrasting emotions for each end of the stick. For example: Fear and Love or Anger and Contentment. They did some writing about each and attached that to the project as well, at each end of the stick. We had some amazing discussions and they looked beautiful and inspiring on the wall. What end of the stick will you focus on? And if you break off the fear end of the stick, is fear still there?

Also at our school we have an amazing Accelerated Reader program, which allows students to read books and then take a comprehension test for the book. It works on a point system. We do cross graded groups so that the students are meeting and making new friends as well.

Another great thing is the Mathletics program which allows students to do math related activities at their own pace and they can even access it at home if they want to work on it there too. From a parent perspective, I love this. Zach and I do about ten minutes a night and he benefits from some one on one time with mom. Google classroom is another amazing tool that we can access from home.

When I'm in any classroom, it's my practice to do a 1-3-5 activity with the students. I do this at the start of the day as I am taking attendance. The students get to tell me and their classmates what their number is on the scale. They each get a chance to have the floor and feel that they are being heard and everyone respects the speaker. One would be that they are having a bad day and five being that it's an awesome day. It is a great tool for me to see who is where as they come into their day and I have heard great things as the kids say stuff like, "Why are you a two today, Ashley? Do you want to play with me at recess?" and "You are a million, Ben? Tell me why?" If there is time, I will often do the activity again after lunch. The kids love it so I keep doing it. I have even had other teachers use it in their classrooms. When something works then it is nice to share the idea.

Another activity that I encourage and incorporate into a day is for students to find the stillness within and then let the writing flow. We would honor one minute of silence followed by writing a quote in their quote book and then reflecting on the quote for about five minutes. The students loved to do this and they were always so proud of the quote books that they created and got to take home at the end of the year. Being a big lover of writing and reading, you could also often find my students laying on the floor or resting in their desks with their heads down as I played some relaxing music which was usually about a five minute piece. Many of the students called it "naptime". Following that they would be given fifteen minutes to free write in their journals. I call it soul journaling. They loved this and I marked some very amazing journals. There are some very talented up and coming writers out there!

Our school also has the Breakfast for Learners program, where members of our community come in and make breakfast for all those students who were too tired, too busy or just didn't feel hungry before they left home. The kids like to socialize while they eat and it just starts the school day off on the right note. Often there are special guests. The local hockey players have been seen stopping by to sign autographs for the students. We have created a wonderful community. Love, love, love it!

One last thing that our school has is the Academy program, where the students in grade seven and eight get to choose interesting classes for themselves based on their interests and the teachers get to teach things that interest them too, so it is a win-win situation. They spend half their afternoon in these chosen activities. It's so cool to see how they learn and grow so much more when they get to have a choice. We all like to have a choice.

Journal entry (15th) - Time flies! Ten years ago I was blessed when a beautiful baby boy was born. I'm proud of the young man you are turning into. HAPPY BIRTHDAY ZACHARY. We had a stay at home day because I needed to help the boys deal with head lice and the flu. Grateful for my washer and dryer today! The things we do for our kids. I remember one time when Jaden was very young and he threw up in his bed and cried out for me in the night. I snuggled him into the top bunk and proceeded to clean the bottom one. As I was doing the laundry, he puked again. There was nowhere to put him, so he decided that he should sleep in the bathtub next to the toilet. Nice problem solving! That worked for me. So he snoozed away in the tub full of blankets for the rest of the night while I did load after load of laundry. It's all worth it.

Journal entry (26th) - As the end of November approaches, we are looking forward to celebrating a great football season at the Spartan Football Banquet and Awards night. Those hard working kids need a big night of celebration like this. They so deserve it! It's so neat to see how much these boys have grown and changed. They are the same sweet personalities in much bigger and stronger bodies!

Reflect - What are you thinking at this very moment? Let go of doubt and let your thoughts flow.

December - DISAPPOINTMENT

I remember to breathe and focus on the stillness within when my desire is to forgive and let go. I make a wish list of what I want and dream BIG. This allows me to find a balance in my body, mind and soul and helps me handle disappointment.

I believe that it's through science that we can prove things but through intuition and creative endeavor that we truly discover. My little science guy, Zachary, has been enlightening me about the feel good hormones, dopamine and serotonin. They are both neurotransmitters and hormones. According to Zach, dopamine increases brain activity in the parts of the brain that are associated with the happy feelings and emotions. Serotonin is found in the gastrointestinal tract, platelets and central nervous system. They are also contributors to the happy feeling. Since we were on the science topic, I asked him, "What is vibrational energy?" He tells me that there is so much to discuss and that everything is energy: the heart pumping, the brain, nuclear power plants that are splitting atoms, sound waves and music. A fortissimo blast from his trombone would be about $1/700^{th}$ of a newton which is also enough to make a snare drum vibrate too. There are quarks and bosons and leptons and the only time that vibration stops is when the temperature drops below absolute zero, which is -278.15 degrees Celsius. There is a weak force which keeps an electron orbiting the nucleus and a strong force that keeps the nucleus itself together. Also, there is a gravitational force and electromagnetic force (negative and positive make this work). He ended the discussion by telling me that I should look up more information about Albert Einstein's unfinished Unified Field

Theory. Albert died before he could finish it and Stephen Hawking is still working with this theory.

Another day, Zach came home from school and I could see the storm cloud over his head. I tried to be as pleasant as possible because we all have bad days. I asked him if everything was okay and he said yes but I could tell he was lying to himself and to me. I let him be, to work through it on his own because very rarely is he ever upset by things this much. I started supper because I could feel he needed some space. As I was humming along to a song on YouTube as I cooked I heard him lose it. He yelled out, "The stupid computer is not working properly. I need a new one! I'm going to save up my Christmas money and buy one after Christmas." The negativity was building. Zach has never been grounded because he is very adaptable, responsible and cooperative but he knows what being grounded is because we have discussed it. We have discussed lots of things because unlike Jaden, Zach likes to talk. So anyway, I say to him quite calmly, "Zach, go to the couch. You are being grounded off your computer." He looked at me and was almost crying as he made his way to the couch. I got the blanket and tucked it around him and gave him a hug then took his socks off and held his feet. I told him that when I felt sick he would rub my feet and it made me feel grounded to the here and now, where there is no problem. He looked at me like I was crazy then started laughing.

Journal entry (15th) - We will be celebrating the holiday season with my beautiful mom, sisters and their amazing families and then be seeing the lights in Airdrie on the way home. I feel so much better than I did last year. It will make me appreciate the joy of the season even more. When we have felt what crappy feels like, then we really appreciate feeling good! Speaking of good, next week Zach will graduate in karate from white belt to white belt with a stripe. Proud of you Zach.

December twenty-sixth on Facebook I posted, "Merry Christmas and Happy New Year to all our family and friends. Peace, Love and Joy from our family to yours. A warm house, movie, popcorn, blankies, hot chocolate, tea and my snuggly boys on this cold Canadian evening. All is well in my world." And it truly is!

Christmas is so much about family for me. We have a fun day out planned. We are heading into Calgary to meet up with mom, my sisters, their kids and hubbies at the Science Center. Zach is so excited about this adventure. He has been researching all the cool things that he will see there.

I am going to be Super lazy today which is like my regular lazy, but I will be wearing a cape. That is all. ☺

It's going to be a Happy, Happy New Year! Looking forward to all the awesome things that will unfold in 2013. Grateful for sooo much. Life is magical with its twists and turns and I wouldn't change a thing.

Reflect - What do you desire and how will you successfully reach this desire?

January - OVERWELMENT

When feeling overwhelmed I take it as a sign that I need to slow down and let the universe help me out. I feel it as a headache, stomach ache and as tightness in my jaw. Does all this stuff need to be done today? No! Some is going to stay on my To Do list for another day and I'm okay with that. For me tapping, breathing deep, getting some exercise and meditating all help me out. When I feel overwhelmed, that is the time that I need to slow down and do something for me or the overwhelment picks up momentum and turns into anxiety and even sometimes fear. I chose to go up the emotional scale and not down it more.

I have on my fridge a poem that was written by one of my very talented students. She wrote it for me when I was sick and I contacted her and she said that I could share it in my book. I hope it inspires you as much as it did me. This is why I teach!

To: Ms. Taylor
Ms. Taylor you inspire me
To be who I want to be,
You teach me to always be strong,
Even when the world feels wrong,
To take challenges as they come,
Because of course there will be some,
I feel special with you,
You've inspired me to do,

Well this you see,
Writing poetry.
By: Abby
I love you Ms. Taylor... You are strong <3
With love: Abby

I was thinking about my friend, Janice, today and how she had said that she was visualizing the boys and me running through a mountain meadow, hand in hand, and my hair was flying in the wind as I ran and we were so free. I have been visualizing that too and today I squeezed my hair into a little ponytail. It's coming along nicely. One day I will manifest that visualization but I still need to let the hair grow some more.

Journal entry (16th) - What a great day to volunteer to tie skates and then to skate with Zach and his classmates. Zach was also picked as one of the Three Stars of the Day. Chosen because of his "can do spirit and great listening skills." That's my boy!

Zach and I just watched a group of seven deer walk past our house and down the road. Majestic, peaceful. All is well! As we watched the group walk so calmly past our house and on down the road, we discussed that the word Silent and Listen have the same letters in them. Also that Reality = Love. Something to think about.

We had a fun day with Zach at his first Karate Tournament. On the way home we talked about our intuition and how when he was in the tournament he just knew some things without even thinking about them. He listened to his heart and trusted what it was saying when he was sparring with others and breaking boards with his hand. We talked about the importance of believing in those feelings and then to move from believing to knowing. Wild animals do it all the time but we as people have forgotten about that ability at times when we use our heads too much. Inspired people, inspire others.

Reflect - Where do you feel overwhelment in your body and how do you release it?

February - FRUSTRATION

I spoke before about a stick project that I have done with my students and this month my stick had frustration at one end and happiness at the other end. Frustration is represented by the color brown in my mind. Not sure why. Maybe it's because brown is a fairly dark color that can go with any other color to give it contrast. I choose to focus more on the end of the stick that represents happiness, love and passion. Speaking of love, I feel the love in my heart as I look at the feisty baby calves that are being born again. Spring is arriving. They are powerful proof for me that miracles do happen and dreams do come true. There is something so amazing about a new life with all its innocence and potential. Happy Super bowl Sunday. Goooo Ravens!

Just when I think things can't get any better, they do! Zach and I were discussing love. We think that love lives in happy hearts and that 'I love you' also means, 'I love how I feel when I think about or am with you'. It's just the short form because people don't want to have to use all those words. We also agreed that trust and love are two very important things that cannot be seen with the eye but must be believed in the heart and felt deep down in your soul. We decided that we should always let our hearts guide us but we have to listen carefully because sometimes it whispers. It is a feeling of warm, personal attachment. Love starts within us and we come to love, not by finding a perfect person or thing but by learning to see the imperfections as perfect. Love people and things as they are and don't judge them. That is a lot of Love. Speaking of love, way to go Zach on taking your science fair project, "The Power of

Love", to the County Science Fair competition. I made a video of his scientific approach and posted it on YouTube so that I could use it when teaching classes (https://youtu.be/br291G70axA). Proud of you buddy!

A Facebook message from my sister Wendy – "BEAUTIFUL WOMAN AND WARRIOR AWARD! The game is as follows … Once selected; you have to choose ten women on Facebook you believe deserve the award, copy and paste this on their wall. You must be honest; it is a way to show your respect and admiration for women who sometimes forget their worth! If you receive it over three times, consider yourself really a beautiful woman and warrior. If you break the game nothing will happen, but it's nice to know that someone appreciates and admires you … and you're a beautiful person inside and out! I chose you!"

Journal entry (18th) - It was a fun Family Day here with a swim and homemade cream puffs. So excited to snuggle down with a new book, tea and blankie. I received a gift that just came in the mail! And it's personalized and signed by the author! I'm so excited to dig right into it and I thank you for sharing your beautiful gift of words and your magnificent gift of friendship, Brian.

This may sound strange but I am grateful for the cancer experience because it has been my biggest growth experience yet and I am thankful because it has shown me the importance and power of life, love, laughter, acceptance, feeling good, appreciation, trust, family, friends and myself. I take nothing for granted anymore. I accepted what it had to teach me and I am moving on with my journey, one step at a time.

Reflect - What color represents frustration for you?

March - IRRITATION

I rritation can be a state of emotions but it can also be a state of inflammation. This is what Jaden had to deal with this month as his appendix became inflamed but lucky for him, it didn't burst. He was happy to have that irritation removed. Also I like to think that without the irritation of a sand grain then there wouldn't be any pearls. I talk more about the pearl in a following chapter.

At the beginning of this month I dropped Zach off at the County Science Fair which was held at the Olds High School. He was so excited and it was neat for me to see some of the wonderful projects and people who make this event happen. A lot of hard work and determination all in one place. Powerful!

Holy Snow! Grateful for my snow shoveling boys. They earned their keep today. Coming together is a beginning. Keeping together is progress. Working together is success.

Journal entry (10th) – Zach and Jaden are both sleeping comfortably and I just got finished talking to the nurse who said that we will be going home today. I was very grateful to the staff at the Olds and Red Deer Hospitals as they so wonderfully helped care for Jaden as he underwent surgery to remove his appendix. He is doing MUCH better and I hope to take him home soon. My brave boy. It was a long day yesterday because the Olds Hospital knew that something was wrong but they couldn't pinpoint it and when they had it narrowed down they decided that Red Deer was the best place for him. In Red Deer he had to undergo more tests and waiting and finally, about eight o'clock, after a long day they did surgery. He told me that he knew how I felt while I played the waiting game for my test results to come back for cancer. He was so happy that they removed it before it burst and the doctor said it was one the verge of it. Zach and I slept on the chairs beside his bed for the night because Zach didn't want to leave Jaden and because Jaden didn't want Zach and me to leave. The nurse said there was a Ronald McDonald House just down the road but the boys wanted to make it into a campout in the hospital and stay together for the night. The nursing staff was so accommodating. It was only one night, thankfully, and my back will be happy to sleep in my own cozy bed tonight.

Enjoyed a really nice visit and coffee/tea with one of my first friends from Sunday School and Kindergarten. It sure didn't feel like all those years had passed us by. Once a friend, always a friend.

I've been continuing my journey to perfect health and abundance in all areas of my life. I have gained back thirty of the forty pounds that I lost and my body is feeling better every day. It takes a long time for the chemo to work its way out of the system. I've been keeping busy subbing and I really am enjoying being around my Deer Meadow family again. I am an 'Essential Piece'. Life is great. Enjoy every day!

My thoughts for today:

> Breathe: 3-4-5
> By letting go of the 'negative' stuff, I open new spaces in my heart to receive the 'amazing stuff'
> LOVE - Living On Vibrational Energy
> Revolution - U R Love
> Be(you) tiful
> Feel Good, Give Thanks, Trust
> Live, Love, Laugh, Let Go
> Look, Listen, Learn, Lead
> Believe
> Power of positive thought
> Music is powerful

Reflect – What are some things that irritate you?

April - IMPATIENCE

Our trip to Radium Hot Springs this month tested my patience. I think that impatience isn't always a bad thing. Actually in small doses it motivates us to learn, grow and create. Jaden turned sixteen this month and the boys and I went to Radium Hot Springs. We had a big learning experience on our trip. I wrote this letter to share with a couple newspapers. I hope you enjoy it...

<u>Lesson Learned</u>

My two boys and I were visiting the Kootenay area during the week of April 22nd to celebrate my older sons 16th birthday as well as my first year of being cancer-free and we were excited about a holiday and much needed break from routines. Our car window was smashed and all our possessions, including my wallet, were stolen from the trunk. This is when the story gets real good…..A chain reaction of love, compassion and kindness unfolds….We are all faced with challenges in our lives. They are the biggest learning experiences. So, you are wondering what we learned? That there are way more helpers than bad guys. We choose to focus on the helpers:

1. Matt - From Vernon told us about our car and then he loaned us $100 to get home.
2. Chris – Gave us his phone number and told us to call if we needed.
3. A girl (I didn't get her name in my confused state) gave us $30 that was left over from her income tax return.

4. A 911 operator who directed us to go to the police station in Invermere.
5. A waitress at Canal Flatts who gave us directions.
6. A firefighter who directed us to the police station, listened to me and sent me on my way with a hug.
7. Cheryl and an officer who assisted us with the police report.
8. Home Hardware in Invermere for supplies to cover my window for our trip back to Alberta.
9. Vince – for helping us cover the window with a good plastic and tape because he saw us struggling to cover the window with a crappy piece of plastic. He must have payed for the plastic too. Beautiful man.
10. Gene – another beautiful man who loaned us $50 and calmed me with his conversation.
11. My Facebook friends who were there with kind words and loving thoughts. Shari posted, "Good friends are like stars. You don't always see them but you know they are always there."
12. Close friends and family who texted support, love and encouragement.
13. Mountain View Credit Union (especially Crystal and Joy) – Closed out my account and got me set up with a new one AND Joy gave me a Nutribar and water when I told her that I had missed lunch.
14. The girl who helped me cancel my Credit card and is sending a new one in the mail.
15. The squirrel for stopping us in our tracks to admire him as we watched him eat a peanut.
16. Our kitty who loved us to pieces when we returned home.
17. Physical and non-physical angels of all kind.
18. Leanne at Double 2 for hooking me up with…..
19. Verla at Sunset Glass.
20. Sue at the Registry Office for her patience as I got my driver's license and birth certificates ordered.

AND I could go on even longer but the paper said it should be under 500 words.

I finish up with my words of inspiration (because I'm a school teacher)

Live fearlessly, Laugh often, Let negative experiences go and Trust that all will unfold in the perfect order for you and when you have to pick up the pieces in your life make sure to:

* See your goal
* Understand the obstacles
* Create a positive mental picture (with feeling)
* Clear your head of self-doubt
* Embrace the challenge
* Stay on track
* Show the world that you can do it

Oh ya and when scary things happen.....look for the kind hearts and hands of the helpers. It makes things feel so much better.

Thank you for reading my thoughts and may your heart be full of love, compassion and kindness today and every day!

Carol

Reflect - What tests your patience?

May - PESSIMISM

O nly a little bit of pessimism this month because I left most of my undesirable outcomes behind me as I brought my thoughts from pessimism to optimism. I now try to view everything as innately good. Pessimism only seems to show up for me if I am digging around too much in the past or the future. When I am in the present moment then it doesn't exist.

I found a piece of writing when I was reading today. It reminded me of the movie *Avatar*, which I love by the way. It was called Magic Words and was of Netsilik origin - Translated by Edward Field. It's awesome and talks about the "oneness" of all things and how we can create our own reality and it resonated with me, so I wrote it out. It helped me work through some pessimism and see the beauty and optimism that life has if we only look. It helped me to see all that was right in this very moment. No worry, no fear, no anger, no stress, just connection and oneness of all things! I even used neat, cursive writing, not my usual scribbling. With red pen, yup! I wanted to make it look fancy.

On the topic of *Avatar*, I remember the time we went with our neighbor, Bob, to see the movie in the theatre and it was playing in 3D so we got those funny glasses and were enjoying the show. Yes, there was popcorn with extra butter. We sat near the front and center, just in case Zach had to leave to go use the bathroom and so we had lots of leg room too. Well, part way through the movie, during the scene when the spirit seeds are landing on Jake, I look over and Zach is standing up reaching to catch the seeds which are coming right out of the screen at us as we watch them. Zach has the spirit. ☺

Journal entry (12th) - We are off to go to Chestermere Lake today to spend time with family for Mother's Day. We will be having a nice Mother's Day lunch at the golf course. Janet said the baby geese have hatched and after lunch maybe we can go for a walk and see them. I'm also feeling really energized today, as I often do on Sunday mornings. I still think it's because of those friends in different churches around town that are praying for us. Prayers are powerful. We are so blessed and surrounded by so many physical and non-physical angels. All is right in my world.

Reflect - What choices have you made that changed your current situation? Give yourself a pat on the back because change is growth and growth is good.

June - BOREDOM

Boredom. Yawn. It's within stillness that we learn so much. We all have feelings of boredom at one time or another but if you quiet your mind and feel with your heart then the boredom transmutes itself and all of a sudden you are standing in the boredom and appreciating it. You say to yourself, "I'm bored and that's great." As a mom of two busy boys, I especially treasure boredom because it means that nothing is scheduled and that anything is possible. I love to go still and just listen.

I read Robert Munch's *Love You Forever* book to each of the boys today. This is one of my favorite books that I have been reading to the boys since they were born. I got a nice, warm hug from each of them. Love my boys...FOREVER!

My friend Jody told me about how she gets email messages from the universe every day that make her smile so I signed up and receive these daily. Some are better than others. Today my message from TUT made me smile big when it told me how much the universe loves me. I knew it already but it was nice to hear it anyway.

Zach and I were 'flying high' today. Literally! We went to the Olds-Didsbury airport because Zach wanted to go flying with the COPA kids program. A wonderful program that is put together to give young people a chance to experience the joy of flight, and that allows senior flyers to share their planes and talents with the younger generation. It's awesome. Zach went for his flight and came back all smiles and full of excitement about his trip and bubbled it over to me. Just as we were about to leave, the organizer asked if there was any parents who wanted to go. Zach said, "Yes! My mom will go!" So away I went for my first flight in a small plane. What a great time, once I got over the nauseous feeling, I enjoyed the true beauty of our planet from the air. I thought to myself, this must be what it's like to fly through the air as an angel. The plane took off in an easterly direction and then travelled along the Queen Elizabeth highway (southbound) for a while. It turned west and flew over Didsbury and all the way out and over our family farm. I took pictures and marveled at how different the farm looks from the air. From a different perspective, it looked like a completely different farm. I gained a new appreciation for it. We turned northward and headed back to Olds where I saw my town and my house from a whole new perspective too. The ground looked very wet because of all the rain we just had. It was saturated and there were puddles everywhere. It really was so beautiful! We headed back and landed safely where Zach was waiting for me with a big smile and said, "Wasn't that just awesome! Aren't you glad you went!" I hugged him and said, "Absolutely." Thanks Zach for helping me see the beauty in it all and for helping me to step out of my comfort zone because that is where the 'good' stuff is!

Reflect - What is something that you discovered about yourself while you sat in stillness and just listened?

July - CONTENTMENT

Zach and I took Frisco for his shots and check-up. He is such a content kitty when he goes there. He doesn't like the cat carrier and the car ride there and back but when he is there, he is good. When we got him home, he went and snuggled with Jaden for a while, then he had a nap and later after his nap he crawled up in my lap. He is so sweet. He rubs his face on me and purrs so loud. He has a very loud motor and really soft fur. His markings are so beautiful. He has been in our lives since the separation and has brought us so much joy and love. I frequently smile and laugh at him as he crawls in my lap, sits on my writing paper, walks on my computer keys and does his own typing for a while, throws my eraser off the desk and onto the floor, crawls up on my tummy when I'm doing Pilates and all the time purring while looking for some attention and love. He stops me in my tracks and makes me smile. He brings me right to the here and now. He is the epitome of contentment. If I come back in another life I would enjoy being a cat that lives in a home that is full of peace and love.

Clean it out and then love and trust. What is in your heart that is not loving? You have to be willing to release judgment and opinion and to forgive or walls are created. There is good in every situation. It will be revealed and it is our interpretation of the situation that really matters. Like attracts like, so be positive. Being a farmer's daughter, I need to harvest the learning from every experience or I will be doomed to repeat it. Let go of resistance. It's like holding a beach ball under the water. Don't do that. The beach ball is meant to be soaring through the air and immersed in the fun of the moment.

I feel safest when I have an open heart and when the love flows through. It is my personal responsibility. If you can't let it go then have one last emotional fling with it then let it go for good. Thank it/them for what it/they did for you. If I ever embark on another intimate relationship then the person will be someone who is for the most part balanced, whole and complete so that we can go forward and dance through the rest of life growing, learning and co-creating together. All baggage released.

Always remember that COMPLAINING makes you a crap magnet. Get off the pain train. Just because the birds are circling your head doesn't mean that you have to let them nest in your hair. But I do remember a time in the barn when I got pooped on by a bird. ☺ Don't invite the negative in; it's a waste of time and energy. I feel so good. I'm going for a walk to bask in this feel good moment and then look forward to a wonderful day with the boys.

Journal entry (31st) - The boys and I are having an amazing summer. We are doing all the cool things we did last year plus more because I'm feeling even better. Calaway Park, the farm, Red Lodge Park and the mountains. One of the highlights so far was a camping trip to Writing On Stone National Park. We went with mom and had a blast. The place had an amazing energy that pulsed through my veins. You could just feel the spirits all around as we walked and talked and played in the river. We would hop in the water at the playground and float downstream and around the bend and end up on the beach where we would hop out and walk back to the playground. The boys worked together and chopped wood and help set up and set down camp. There is something very cozy about being in a tent and sleeping so close to the ones you love. The scenery was breathtaking too. Being in nature inspires me. I definitely want to go back. Thanks for coming with us mom. Love you!

Reflect - What makes you content? Now go do that.

August - HOPEFULNESS

I love summer! It is a time to renew and recharge so that I can focus on the hopefulness that resides within me. It gives me time to go through things and really appreciate them. Lovingly, I was organizing and sorting and came across an envelope with cards that I had saved from when I was sick and I really enjoyed reading these again. I'm glad I kept them. They are love notes from friends. They are love notes that have prompted hope within me. I will share some today...

- "Dearest Carol. I put together this little care package with you in mind. Two of my favorite things is a long, hot bath followed by a wonderful movie! In addition, I have found that journaling helps me see things clearer when the days are dark. And finally ~ have Faith. My favorite passage is Jeremiah 29:11. Check it out and have faith that God's plan for you includes watching your boys grow up, alongside their beautiful mother. With love, Lori xo"

- "Here's a little get well note, to add sunshine to your day... with a wish that you'll soon get well and always stay that way. My dearest, that is my wish for you! A special angel just for you. Carol, whenever we are camping or hiking... if you find a rock with a hole in it, it means 'Good luck'. Keep it, put it in your pocket. And then you find yourself returning to your pocket just to run your fingers over the surface of your rock! This stone too, can be put in your pocket for solace, strength and for peace and harmony in your life. Just put your hand in your pocket and feel the strength!! Take care. Love Paulette xo"

- "Healing takes time, so be patient. Healing takes effort, so think positive thoughts. Healing also takes warm wishes from people who care – and you have plenty of those! We are thinking about you. Take care of yourself. Love you. Calvin, Elaine, Tammy & Ethan"

- "What an amazing miracle to see... a butterfly unfold its wings for the first time. During those difficult days, we may discover wings we never knew we had... the beautiful strength within. Dearest Carol, Just a few words of encouragement and heartfelt thoughts during this challenging time. My thoughts are often and will often be with you over this next period of time. Take care. All my best, Char"

- "Courage... is not the absence of fear or despair, but, the strength to conquer them. Dearest Carol, I just wanted to take a moment to tell you how much you are loved. I cannot imagine the thoughts that will be racing through your mind right now. But your friends at Deer Meadow consider you a treasured part of the family. We will do everything possible to care for you and the boys. I promise. Now,,, that is what DMS thinks of you - but I want to tell you what our family thinks of you. My children and I are blessed to have you as a part of our lives. Justin thinks you are a really 'cool sub'. But you have enriched Ashley's life - you made a difference in her world. You teaching her (primarily in Gr. 6) is one of her most valued experiences. She lists you as one of her all-time favorite teachers. As her mother, I cannot thank you enough for being such an amazing role model for my daughter. Now... my turn! Carol - you are such an extraordinary, courageous woman. I look at the challenges that life has given you. And yet, you hold your head up, you face each day and you battle on. You are one of the most gentle, genuine, hard-working and loving persons I know. I feel so lucky to call you my friend. Remember the tea bag, my darling friend. I am confident of your true strength. I will do anything and everything possible to help and support you and the boys. Hang in there. You can beat this. I am surrounding you with extra angels! Lotsa Love, Lori xo P.S. Hopefully this $ will help as any unexpected expenses arise."

- "Thoughts as warm as sunlight spilling through a window are with you today. And every day! Your strength and beautiful spirit inspires me daily. All my thoughts and prayers. Keara"

- "Remembering special people like you is one of the nicest things about Thanksgiving (life). You bring so much love and happiness to so many people - please accept this tiny bit in return! Jaden, you are a wonderful young man. I know, because your mom tells me so every time we talk! Zachary, you are a very special young man! I know you are being a great help for mom! Thinking of you, Amy"

- "Abundant love surrounds you. You've got this! You are the winner! Fight hard & hugs will be abundant when you need them. The Smith Gang

  PS - You are an inspiration for us all and I hope I can be half as passionate and caring while teaching as you! Keep shining your beautiful light! Hayley - Big bear hug"

- "A hug and a prayer... that you feel better soon. Wishing you a quick recovery & healing in every way. Hugs, Janice"

- "Hair is so overrated. With or without it, you're gorgeous no matter what! Here is a little something to keep your fingers warm as you go out for walks in your funky hats! I am so proud of you. You are in my thoughts and prayers always!! Much love, Lori xo"

I feel that many themes run through my story. One is the powerful role that my love, hopefulness and affection play in my family as we are coping with the challenges of cancer and single parenting. Another is the importance of the acceptance of suffering and the giving up of resistance. There is not much we can do about our situations, but, as I reveal in my story, accepting the condition in which we find ourselves can be a far more positive approach in the long run.

I have been spending lots of time in my yard these ideal summer days because the fruits in my yard are ready to harvest. I have picked buckets and buckets of cherries and put them in the freezer so that I have cherries all winter. Also, this year my apple tree produced an abundant amount of apples. What we didn't eat fresh I made into apple sauce and put that in the freezer too. Yummy! We reap what we sow.

Journal entry (29th) - That was an amazing summer. We had so much fun that it just flew by. This month we had backyard fires, wiener roasts and S'mores. Zach loved the sparklers I bought and it was so nice to just sit by the fire and stare at the flames as they danced above the wood, with the sparks flying up and out and I had no urge to grab a coal and throw it either. ☺ The smell reminded me of fires past and good memories. Yes, spent many nights sitting by the fire meditating. Also, this month we went roller blading, hung out at the park and rode our bikes lots. Zach has a big bike now so he was learning to keep the balance. Yes balance, that is a good topic. Zach discovered that he can lean a bit either way and he is okay as long as he keeps moving but there is no balance and usually a crash happens when you stop moving or if you lean too far to the right or the left. We made cookies, slept on the back deck under the stars. Zach and I saw the ISS travelling across the sky when we were star gazing and I went to the dinner theatre with mom. We went to Burntstick Lake and swam in the water and watched the geese with their new babies. I love it there just hanging out on the boat dock being in the moment. Janet and Perry hosted the annual swimming pool/birthday party for my amazing nieces and we got to hang out and feel the love of family. The boys spent hours in Auntie Janet's pool.

Jaden took his driver training and is becoming a competent driver. I on the other hand did not do so well. Change takes a while to sink in for me. One day Jaden was driving and I saw the car in front of us braking and being the stress case that I can be I shouted, "BRAKES! BRAKES! BRAKES!" Jaden looked over calmly and said to me, "It's okay, I saw him." Zach burst out laughing in the back seat and then Jaden and I did too. Good times and believe me, they won't let me live it down. I have been driving along a few times this month already and I hear Jaden or Zach yell for no reason, "BRAKES! BRAKES! BRAKES!" Also, football season has started again and I'm happy to reconnect with my football family. Such good times, such great people!

Reflect - Write down as many questions as you can then go back and answer your own questions.

September - ACCEPTANCE

Acceptance – Yes – This is yummy! When I released resistance this is the emotion that flooded in. I was lucky to experience lots of acceptance this month. There was the feeling of acceptance of self and of all that is. Acceptance goes hand in hand with unconditional love. First for yourself then you can give to others. Love as I understand it for me - Unconditional connection and things that make you feel good, just as they are, drawing out the love that is within us. Love is how the body, mind and soul react to those connections. Is it a positive reaction? Then that is love. Love is from within and if you choose to share your gift then that is your choice. It's a gift that you will always grow from and so will others. So really it is a gift to all. Be loving. And you may ask, so what about the things that make us feel negative? I believe those are the learning/growth experiences. Love them too. Look at them, learn from them, then let them go and focus on what you want. Loving others is easy when you love yourself.

Journal entry (4th) - The words inside my Jones Soda lid gave me a message. I wonder what is coming my way. "A tantalizing prospect will come your way." I love surprises.

I found some more get well cards/love letters of hope and acceptance from friends. These just warm my heart!

- "Dear Carol, A period of trial and tribulations has come to an end. Your positive manner and strength of character got you through. Now, let's celebrate. May you enjoy our small gift and have many wonderful days ahead. Love, Char and Jan"

- "Dear Carol & Boys, In celebration of the end of your treatments! Enjoy our gift with your boys as you continue to heal and celebrate each day. With love, Some friends"
- "If I forget to tell you Carol, or I miss seeing you, I wish you a great holiday with the boys and your sister and her family! I'll be thinking of you - xxxoxxx. Remember we are still going to sit in your backyard and smell the sweet blossoms on your trees. Friends Forever, Paulette"
- "This is Bell Rock near Sedona (on the front of the card). Janet and I both felt a strong pull towards it. We said next time we would like to hike there and experience it's vortexes. I hope you will be able to get close up and personal with this place. I will be with you in spirit (as always). Mom"

My day to day things just make life feel so right. Looking forward to a nice weekend. Sleeping in then a football game in Olds tomorrow and boating on Dickson Dam on Sunday with our neighbor, Marcel. Life is good. I plan on getting up on the water skis and seeing how long I can hang on. The boys are looking forward to tubing. Fun in the sun!

School is back in and I have a contract at my wonderful school teaching grade seven science. The class is amazing and I'm looking forward to learning and growing with this group all year and I have the best team teaching partner ever, Lori. Speaking of Lori, I remember a time when I had just separated from Darrell and was adjusting to the change and Lori saw that I was a little down at work. She gave me a teabag and told me to think of myself as a teabag. The longer I steep the stronger I get. Lori was also there for me when I was going through chemo. She came over with homemade chicken noodle soup and other goodies to brighten our day.

My boys are happily settled into grade eleven for Jaden and grade five for Zach. The time is going fast. Babies no more. Just kidding, they will always be my babies. Football has started for Jaden and he is determined to have an injury free year. He's a good manifester, just like his mom and I bet he will. It has been great hanging out with my football family again.

Journal entry (24th) - I started doing some acupuncture at The Little Shop of Healers in town. I love it. I have also been making time for massages. I need to keep my bucket full. I've been eating well and exercising and getting lots of sleep. I've also been learning so much. Thankful for books and the internet. There is homework to do and supper to be made and marking to do so I will sign off with LOVE.

Reflect - What brings you to a place of unconditional love and acceptance?

October - OPTIMISM

Optimism - I hung out here a lot this month. I believe that optimism is vital to success and that it's the foundation for progress. Yes for courage and true progress. I watched *Nemo* with Zach today. Dori is one of the most optimistic fish I know! "Just keep swimming, swimming, swimming. What do we do? We swim and swim."

Journal entry (5th) - A fun football weekend. The Spartans won against Brooks last night, forty nine to seven and today they play a charity game, in Olds, with the Olds RCMP and Stampeders Alumni. It's a touch football game; we didn't want our Spartans teaching the RCMP any new takedown moves. Also, Jaden brought home the mechanical/learning baby, TJ, that's required for his CALM class. Jaden has to change it, feed it, burp it and love it. He keeps it for two days and has had it for six hours and has decided that he is not having a baby for a LONG time. I'm good with that. ☺ What a great project!

Zach made me a bracelet when he was younger. I actually remember when he made it. It was the time that we stayed at Lake Louise with Irene. On that trip we stopped at the candy store in Banff and Irene bought the boys the biggest jaw breakers she could find. The boys licked on those for years. We took those jaw breakers to Lake Louise where we discovered that the Chateau was one of the most amazing hotels that we ever stayed at. Wonderful view, all nested in the mountains, delicious food, a big pool area, walking paths and there was a gem shop right in the hotel. We spent hours among the beautiful energy of the crystals. Zach especially loved the huge amethyst. Anyway, back to Zach, he made me the bracelet with beads and tiny letters that spelled MOM and when he gave it to me, he said, "Look! MOM upside down is WOW." I still keep that bracelet in my bedroom because it holds so many great memories.

Because we saw pearls in the gem shop at Lake Louise, I was also thinking about pearls and how cool it is that they start as a tiny grain of irritating sand and grow into something exquisite. There is so much optimism and change with them. Change is good because change is growth. There was something wrong in my marriage and I knew I had to change it. Similarly, there was something wrong in my body and I had to change that too. All this change causes huge and rapid growth. When you go through something like this, it's important to first find what caused it then build from there. Find the small irritating grain of sand that then grows protective layers to keep the oyster from being irritated. For me, my grain of sand was stress, negativity, anger and the uncertainty of divorce. That's what brought cancer tumors for me, was my cause, and just like the oyster puts the pearl coating on the sand grain; my body was creating a thick tumor casing to contain the spread of the cancer. We all have cancer in our bodies but it only appears as a tumor when we harbor the conditions to allow it to grow. I had all those conditions. It was a hard pill to swallow that I had created the chaos in my body but once I did then I knew I could also change things and prevent it from happening again.

My advice for others:

1. Fill up your bucket first! Take care of yourself. If you are feeling like you need something, you probably do. Listen.
2. Find balance in your life. Givers who give and give until you have nothing left. You have to make that time for yourself.
3. Look within. See where you need to grow. We all have different journeys.
4. Listen to your heart. If you don't want to do something, then don't. Don't guilt yourself into something. Listen to

your impulse, your instinct, your intuition and go with that. If something sounds good, do that.

5. Let life unfold naturally. Those are the doors that you go to. If you are trying to kick down a door, make something happen then that means you aren't supposed to go there. Just relax and walk away. Another door will open. Walk through.

Proud mom today. Zach has collected just under $1000 in pledges from family, friends and neighbors and today his hair comes off at the Deer Meadow Head shave for cancer event. That's my boy. Also, we've been Boo'ed. It's so much fun living in a small town. Tonight it's Zach's turn to run around the neighborhood and leave surprises for neighbors. Jaden said it's like "Nicky Nicky Nine Doors" except you actually leave a special treat when you ring the doorbell and then run. It was so much fun to hide in the bushes and watch Zach as he would deliver the surprises. A real fun memory with my little man.

Journal entry (28th) – A busy, busy football month. Love it. Jaden played at McMann Stadium. It was cool to see our small town boys playing such a great game in the big Stadium. I see great things in football for a lot of these boys. Olds has football talent! Also, I was digging through my cedar chest one day and came across a bean pin that had a smiley face and found a note that I had written. Bob, my neighbor and friend gave me the bean and I wrote a note back to him saying, "The more I think about the bean the more special it is. Thank you. You want me to be a survivor because that's what a bean is. They have so much potential and can grow so much. Thanks again for being an awesome human bean."

As I write today, I take the good with the bad. It is what it is. There are moments when I feel negative emotions and that isn't a bad thing, it's a good thing. In my negative emotion moments I launch powerful rockets of desire. I ask very powerfully for the rightness to appear. It's like snatching victory from the jaws of defeat. I have discovered that I shine in a crisis and I think that's because the crisis makes me focus. When it really matters then I focus on the rightness in the situation. That's why so much of my writing has the day-to-day happenings because that is where the rightness and beauty is for me. When I was sick I didn't want to read about sick people, I wanted to read about success. There were a lot of stories of sickness, suffering and slow death and I avoided those. There were far fewer success stories but I searched them out. Louise Hay and Kris Carr were two such people who inspired me. I decided that if I write my story then it will be a story of success, not a story of suffering. It will uplift the reader not drag them down further. It will show that the day-to-day is where the good stuff happens. It will help bring them right here, right now.

Reflect - What have you achieved because you had an optimistic attitude?

November - POSITIVE EXPECTATION

I'm glad I chose to have positive expectations and not listen to the negative ones. This month I wrote out all my hopes and dreams and special words and assembled them into a heart shape so that on days when my positive expectation is dwindling then I can pull out my creative heart drawing and focus on all of the positives. I glued the heart to a pink piece of paper and I just keep adding words as they come to me. I'll keep my little positive expectation treasure forever.

I feel energized. It must be Sunday! ☺ I also had some free time today and was digging around in stuff from the past and found something I had written back when I was sick. It said, "Just doing laundry is so hard. I can't believe how much effort it takes to just walk up the stairs! One step at a time... I need a nap!" That was then and this is now. Feeling thankful! I also found a list that I had made when chemo brain had fully kicked in. It said, "Eat, sleep, breathe, hug the boys and do Pilates".

Wishing a Happy Eleventh Birthday to my big little man – Zachary, you are growing so fast and you make me proud every day! Sometimes you will never know the true value of a moment until it becomes a memory. There is no future to predict. It's right here. No knowledge to know. It's known now. No love to find because love is here. All there is to do is to enjoy the ride and think with intuition because the basis of thinking is intuition. Feelings and intuition are one and a person never goes wrong following his feelings. With that being said, follow your heart Zach, on your birthday and always.

Journal entry (19th) - It was a crazy day at school. Our field trip busses had to return home after we headed out on bad roads then we had an unexpected fire drill. Now my class is totally unfocussed. Is it a full moon? It's -35 C with a wind-chill. Brrrr! Stay warm today.

Last week was a big week with a lot of medical tests and today I got the call confirming what I already knew in my heart. It was kind of like waiting for test results in school when I knew in my heart that I had aced the tests. My doctor called because she just wanted to let me know that all my tests came back good. She told me that she would see me in a year. THAT was a nice call to get! Positive expectations had a lot to do with this. All is well in my world and I'm looking forward to the best year yet. 2014 here I come. When I posted this wonderful information on Facebook I received 79 likes. People love to hear good heartwarming news.

This poem by Gerald Rogers really inspires and resonates with me and when I read it, I get goose bumps, so I knew that I had to include it in my book. Thanks Gerald.

Courage

The wind, the sun, the rain
The force of the raging storm
That at times seem they will never end
Have beaten against her heart

Yet still she stands

In the shadow of death
She has lost those she loves most
With sickness and sorrow
Haunting her weary path

Yet still she stands

Abandoned by those
Who should've stood by forever
And left alone to face the
Cold unrelenting darkness

Yet still she stands

She was not born a warrior
With a sword or shield to fight
Yet unflinching she faces her battle
Day by day defending those she loves

And Still she stands

She does not resent her hardships
But embraces them with calm knowing
That they are gifts which have made her richer
Stronger in body and soul

She was not born to wither
Not born to hide
She was not born to cower
From the threats that life would throw

No.
She was born to rise.
She was born to shine.

A goddess in the shaping
Like a masterpiece buried in stone
Each knock of life's sharp chisel
Each of the hammers blows
Bringing her a little closer
To her perfection.

And someday, when the time is right,
And when her work is done
She will stand in glory
As others stand in awe.

She is courage.

Reflect - Make a positive expectation wheel for yourself. Put the word "Courage" in the middle and draw a circle around it. Now write down as many positive things as you can about yourself.

December - BELIEF

I believe that it's going to be a wonderful, peaceful, joyful, loving month and I invite you to share the Christmas joy with me. For me, December has always been about belief and actually I like to take that believe with me throughout the year. If I can conceive an idea and really believe it, then I know I can achieve it. Zach and I decided to achieve a great day as we bundled up and walked to school today. A snow day here and only 1/3 of my grade seven class made it to school because of the blizzard. It was a movie day with computer time and a double gym period for the class and some extra prep time for me. Jaden is at home shoveling and doing dishes because the busses weren't running.

So after school the next day, I was outside shoveling the mountain of snow in front of my house because all Jaden's hard work yesterday had blown in and because I needed a place for my family to park next weekend, when they come here for Christmas. Then out of the blue a grader comes to help. The Universe loves me. Thank you town of Olds grader driver.

On the eleventh, a cool alignment number happened, 11-12-13: The eleventh of the twelfth month of 2013. All is in alignment. Speaking of alignment makes me think of balance again. I believe that we need to find balance between 'doing' and 'being'. It needs to be an inspired doing and not a forced doing. There have been many doors that I have tried to kick down and when I do that, it only hurts my toes. It's much better to just walk away and see what door opens as you walk by and you may be pleasantly surprised with all the light and love that comes out of the door that opens easily.

Journal entry (15ᵗʰ) - Feeling inspired to write because it's Sunday again and because we had Christmas supper at my house yesterday and my quiet, peaceful home was turned into a beautiful flurry of laughter, noise, music, food and fun. I loved the fishing game mom and so did the boys. I didn't have the energy to cook for everyone so we all went out for Chinese smorgasbord and then came back to my house for presents. After that we went over to the school and played in the gym and on the climbing wall. We checked out my classroom, where I live during the week. You should have seen Riley's face and heard her say, "Unnnnncle Perry.. UHHHH. No, No, No" when Perry picked up a whiteboard marker and started drawing on the Interactive Smart board. It all came off with a little elbow grease. My grade seven class and Lori won't even be able to tell. My bucket is full!

There is no better than here. What you make of your life is up to you. Others are only mirrors of you and there are no mistakes - only lessons. Life of course will always give us lessons so keep learning because if you don't learn then the lesson will keep repeating itself until you learn it. And learning never ends so like I said, what you make of your life is up to you. All your answers lie inside you. Bananas, books, coconuts, pineapples, dragon fruit and the fridge, all have one thing in common. It's what's INSIDE that counts! $h!T Happens - deal with it! So today, I am making my day a good one. The tree has presents for the boys, Frisco is under it playing with a ribbon and the boys and I are happy and healthy. JOY. LOVE. PEACE!

Journal entry (26ᵗʰ) - We went to the Airdrie Festival of lights with mom today. The lights were so amazingly enticing and I smiled and took pictures of the boys and mom as they were showered in the dazzling lights. Good times and in a couple days we are off to play in our own bounteous Rocky Mountains. Do what you love and love what you do.

Here is my wish for you. I wish for peace of mind. I wish for prosperity through the year. I wish for happiness that multiplies. I wish for great health for you and yours. I wish for fun around every corner. I wish for the energy to chase your dreams and last but not least I wish for joy to fill your holidays and that you can take that feeling into the New Year!

Reflect - What do you believe?

January - ENTHUSIASM

I feel enthusiastic about the New Year! Even if you fail at something, if you can do it with enthusiasm then you learn so much. In about a month, we will be in Florida and before that time we are going skiing to Nakiska, and Zach will be participating in the science fair. Life is great and I am excited about all the wonderful things that are unfolding in my life.

Learning, growing, changing, loving. I saw a lava lamp today and... I want one! They are so cool. They take a while to heat up but once they do, watch out because you can't stop them. The beauty is breathtaking.

Journal entry (22nd) - My Facebook friend, Yvonne, always posts cool and beautiful things on Facebook and I always think it's awesome when she tags me in her posts. My inbox is full of hearts, gratitude and love. She always brings a love fest to my day when she does that. Thanks Yvonne!

I went for a drive today and love was driving. I stopped and did some writing when I was parked at the top of a hill. I listened to my fear and I let it sit in the backseat. When I make a decision I don't worry about what might happen if I chose wrongly. I trust my heart to make choices so that I don't feel like I'm standing at the bottom of the hill and my car is at the top in neutral waiting to be bumped so it can run me over. When I feel anxiety holding me back, I leap forward and trust. Think of it, as if your car is in neutral and is about to roll down the hill and you get out in front of it and let it bump up against you. All is ok. There isn't a lot of momentum there yet but if you let the anxiety carry you away then there is a lot of momentum.

So to compare, you wouldn't want to stop your car from the bottom of the hill: that would not be pretty. Of course as humans we are programmed with fear. It's our fight-or-flight instinct that's designed to keep us safe in the face of danger. Between our biology and our conditioning, just turn on the nightly news, it's no wonder fear drives many of our decisions. The big problem is that fear is a terrible driver who steers us away from opportunities and causes us to miss out on what's really important for our lives. Letting fear/anxiety drive constricts our sense of self and is the greatest source of suffering in our lives. Fear is necessary for the drive but make sure it's in the backseat and tell it not to be a backseat driver because love is at the wheel and will make the decisions. Acknowledge fear but don't let it drive. Keep love at the wheel and let it be your GPS to take you where you need to go. Ready, set, go. Turn the ignition, put it in drive and accelerate.

It was a divine night to stargaze, with the telescope, at Deer Meadow Park. We saw Orion, the Big Dipper, Jupiter, Sirius and many more cool things. The universe is so vast and angelic and mysterious. Zach and I felt very small and it also made us remember the movie, *Horton Hears a Who*. There is so much we can't explain and that's ok because life would be boring if we knew it all. We came home after and did some more research about the stars and then snuggled in and watched some T.V. and ate popcorn. I love my life.

Journal entry (29th) - I am lucky to be science fair coordinator at Deer Meadow this year. Thanks to all the amazing parents and teachers, in my community, who have inspired and supported our students' interest in the science fair. We have 33 participants this year and I think that is wonderful. 33 is an awesome number. Here at Deer Meadow we encourage our amazing science geeks. Zach said that he likes to be a science geek because all the people who have done great things in science and in other areas too were considered outcasts or geeks at one time or another. Just to name a few of Zach's favorites: The Wright Brothers and their flying machine, Albert Einstein and his theories of relativity, Nikola Tesla and his alternating current system and even Steven Hawking and his theories on black holes and radiation. They were all geeks and look where being a geek got them.

Also at the Meadow there was a ski trip. The boys and I rode the bus up to Nakiska with all the other Deer Meadow crew and had a wonderful day skiing. The boys and I let go of a lot of resistance, fears, worries and apprehension as we swooshed down the slopes and enjoyed the fun filled, joyful day. Just like a good meal, fruits on a tree or really anything that we create that is great - like a ski day, love and energy needs to be put into them to make them go from being just okay to being awesome. The real good things take time. Thanks Jeff for organizing this. I love my Deer Meadow family.

Reflect - Write about something that you have achieved when you failed with enthusiasm.

February - EAGERNESS

I've been waking up in the mornings these days full of eagerness and energy with the knowing inside me that great things are ahead for the boys and me. I'm happy where I am and eager for more. Leaders are always readers. Books are magic. Books are powerful. Books cause us to visualize some great things so that we can eagerly achieve them. Read success stories. They are the best!

That was then, this is now. I was standing at the kitchen sink cleaning a big pile of dishes and thought to myself how this pile would have stressed me out three years ago and I would have been rushing through to get on to the next chore. But not now - now I enjoy the feeling of the warm water on my hands and the smell of the soap and the sound of Zach talking on the phone to his friend in the background. I hear Jaden laughing downstairs as he visits with his friends online. The kettle is just about to whistle so I can make a tea, I have the nature channel on T.V. and I can just feel that spring is very soon to arrive and that I am so very glad to be alive. There is something so pleasing about a warm spring day after a long cold harsh winter. Contrast – gotta love it.

It has been two years since my last chemo treatment and with every passing day I am grateful that I focussed on my goal of good health and not on the obstacles. I knew that I would only be given what I could handle. I'm also grateful that I took the leap of faith and trusted in the process even when I couldn't see the end result. It is wonderful to be living a fun, balanced and healthy life. You can create as you wait.

I'm enjoying my part time work with my Deer Meadow family. It is a perfect balance for me right now. I can spend time with my grade seven science classes and if I feel like it then I can fill in the extra time with subbing. It's just enough work that I'm feeling in harmony with my home and work life. I have lots of time for work and play. I have ample time to enjoy the boys every day as well as doing some writing. 'Smiling Single Mom' - this came to me one morning so I started up a new Facebook page and was inspired to do some writing. Could it maybe be a book?

Journal entry (8th) - February brought Zach to another science fair. Zachary is my science guy. His eagerness to learn and grow and share is an inspiration to me. I'm so proud of him and it is exciting for me to watch his enthusiasm as he works on his project and log book and then tells me all about how this is going to change the world in the future. He will do great things in science, I just know it!

I love travelling. It gives me a whole new perspective on things and puts me completely in the moment. My senses feel so keen and everything just seems more alive and brilliant. It brings out the eagerness in me. This is the short version of what I wrote in my journal. Thanks for coming with me on this little get away.

Trip to Cocoa Beach

Valentine's Day came and went and what better way to celebrate than to be in Florida staying at Cocoa Beach. Doubletree by Hilton was a wonderful home for a week. We even got upgraded rooms and warm cookies when we arrived. We had been planning and eagerly anticipating this trip for six months. Good things take time! We drew hearts in the sand and enjoyed the sound of the waves as they rolled in and out. It is so cool how for every wave that comes in another one goes out. Such a tantalizing dance the water does. Just like the waves, all good things are flowing to the boys and me. What we give out comes back. The Universe/God/Angels/Source has us covered. In the mornings the boys would sleep late and I would get up early and drink tea and watch the sunrise, which by the way was really something to see. The sun rising and slowly dawning on a new and beautiful day. Wow, just wow! The colors were amazing and stopped me in my tracks each morning. I did a meditation while I was there by Janet Attwood. It gave the message - I want for you what you want for you, and this meant a lot at the time because I do believe that the universe does want for me what I want for me.

We made some wonderful memories at Cocoa Beach. I would love to go back there one day and kayak, play with jellyfish, swim in the ocean, see wild dolphins jumping in the ocean, take a long walk down to the pier, have tea with my friend Don, swim in the pool, go to Kennedy Space Center and play on the beach another time. Oh and the Slurpee's by the pool that were Pina Colada and strawberry flavored. Yum. One evening when Wendy, Mike and the kids stopped by for a visit, they also thought the Slurpee's by the pool were yummy. That night, we all enjoyed the moon rise over the ocean as we hiked on the beach. We took some fun family pictures. The day we were leaving some splendid little birds came by and ate sunflower seeds off our balcony. It was like they were saying to us, "I hope you made some wonderful memories in sunny Florida. Please take a piece of us in your hearts as you return home." Speaking of birds and flying, Zach loves airplanes so he was thrilled that we had lots of changing of flights and he got to feel take-off and landing lots of times. Zach said, "The world is a small place when you really think about it."

The only thing that I would do differently next time would be to get a GPS in the rental car so that I don't get lost trying to find the hotel. My internal GPS didn't work to find the hotel and we had to ask for directions. The boys will always remember this trip. I took tones of pictures so that I can go there in my head when I need a mini holiday. The boys and I are starting to plan an adventure for next year. I'm eager to start manifesting a ski trip to our very own majestic Rocky Mountains. Jaden suggests Lake Louise.

Reflect - Wake up tomorrow and before you get out of bed feel excitement and eagerness for your day.

March - HAPPINESS

We all strive for happiness. It is what we are all wanting deep down. Happiness transpires for me when what I think, what I say and what I do are in harmony. This made me happy - Zach and I watched a couple movies this weekend on the PVR. And of course there was lots of popcorn with extra butter. The movies were called, *Ella Enchanted* and *Jinxed*. In both movies, a looming curse had to be overcome. Zach and I concluded that we are all cursed; it's just how we deal with the curse that matters. Both girls in the movies learned to overcome the thing that controlled them and found freedom within themselves. We also discussed that all really good movies are well balanced. There is some love, some inspirational stuff, a conflict, it's funny and makes us laugh. Always in the end a lesson is learned. Zach and I decided that we have a story that is worth making a movie about. We also decided that the writers would have to add more funny stuff to make it even better.

Zach and I put on some music today and were dancing around upstairs, loving life with not a care in the world and singing ... yes, there was off key singing as well. We were rocking it to Pharrell Williams, "Happy" song. We must have made a bit too much noise because we looked over and Jaden was standing at the stairs shaking his head and smiling. I saw the, 'I don't know you people' - expression on his face. He gave me a hug and went back to his bedroom. It's so important to just dance your way through life and do things that feel good because those things also advance you in life.

Zach said to me, "I think that pain is what happens when weakness leaves our bodies and gets replaced with strength."

Sometimes he says things that just knock me on my butt. He is so wise for his years. Or maybe he picked up the quote from playing 'Team Fortress 2'? Either way, it meant a lot to me!

Journal entry (12th) - Happy Birthday Mom. I Love you. You always called me your 'big helper' when I was growing up because I was the oldest of us three girls and indeed I was a big helper for you. Now I'm a mom, teacher and writer and I still feel that I am a 'big helper'. Thank you for instilling that in me.

I found an old piece of paper as I was trying to organize my cedar chest and it said, "Breathe and focus on what you want and not on what you have because it takes a while for the good stuff to manifest." True that!

We often change because we have no choice. When our hearts ache and we cling to the past, we create pain for ourselves inside and outside. As well, we create pain for all those around us that we love. It's sad really. And once we realize how nice it is to be pain-free then we fall more deeply in love with this moment and with ourselves. This in turn creates love for all those around us too!

Reflect - What makes you happy? Go do it.

April - PASSION

This emotion reminds me of Jaden because this month he turns seventeen and the world is his oyster. He has a passion for life and learning and wants to go to college and study Instrumentation so he can work in the oilfield or whatever job he is passionate about. There are so many opportunities with this career choice. There is a 94% employment rate when he gets done his college training. I have always told him that he can do or be anything he wants if he sets his mind to it and his passion for life and learning is proving that he can. He has been raised with the idea to follow his passion and to be prepared to work hard and to not let anyone or anything limit his dreams. Dream Big then go live it. I know in my heart that he will get in.

I have had a few people asking for my advice about problems so I wrote this up. I hope that it helps all who read it. It just flowed right out the pencil. It was like God was writing it for me. Enjoy.

Believe

As you know....I like to express myself through words and as I sit here sipping tea, I feel the need to listen to my heart and write this letter. I love you and I believe in you and I am one of your support people...in the same way that when I was sick you were there for me as you loved me, believed in me and supported me. I just wanted to share the six things that helped me beat cancer in hopes that my list can help you too.

1. Believe - I believed with all my heart, mind and body that I would get through it. I had a dream and a burning desire to achieve it!

2. Support - I reached out and trusted in my support people - my family, my friends, my doctors. I surrounded my world of healing in a bubble of love. I saw all the beautiful things that surrounded me and was very thankful for them.

3. Intuition - I listened to my heart. If something felt wrong, I listened. This is why surgery and chemo felt right for me but radiation and five years of drugs did not. I did the Sway Test on many things and today I have a pendulum that helps me listen to my intuition.

4. Cause - This was the hardest step of all for me because it meant digging into my feelings and asking what I could do to fix things. For me, there was a lot of resistance that I had to let go because all the negative emotions cause stress and I think stress was my cause. Everybody has a different cause and only they can find it. I support you in finding your cause.

5. Prevention - This is the "What can I do?" to keep this situation from occurring again. This is where your action plan comes into place. So for me, my work became a goal to reduce stress in my life through many ways and I am still learning new things every day. I do things every day to fill up my bucket because I realized that if my bucket is empty then I am no good to anyone. I could write for pages and pages on this step because it's my favorite and because it's ever changing.

6. Surrender - Forgive and move forward. Have faith and know that you are surrounded by angels of all kinds. In short "Let Go and Let God".

I hope this helps in some way for you and just know that the boys and I and many, many more that surround you right now love you, believe in you and support you. Now for my question - Do you believe? Because I think that miracles happen for those who believe.

Much Love

Carol

Reflect - What lights your passion on fire?

May - JOY

May is my month of Joy. I have been carrying it with me since Christmas and it's always there to some degree. And it's Happy Birthday to me AGAIN. It's funny how something as simple as a birthday can bring such great joy. I truly value each year that I am here on this earth. To celebrate, I went for my usual walk today but it was full of inspiration and beauty - even more than usual. The birds were busy doing their bird things and making lots of pretty noises and I found a feather. People who saw me probably thought I was crazy as I would stop dead in my tracks and pull out my notebook and start writing then tuck it back in my pocket and walk on. I go through the park that has lots of trees because I like to walk as far away from the cars and traffic as possible. There is a tree there that I hug when I go past it - my hugging tree. It's on the leading edge of the forest and there is lots of growth and change happening just to the west of it. Baby trees are popping up and small bushes are getting bigger. Yes, I hug trees and so does Zach. We believe that they have root connections that they communicate with too. The movie, *Avatar*, made a big impression on us. So, as I walk I also go past the lake and then I head through the new development area where there are lots of new houses. Lots of growth and change has happened in this area over the past three years. There is a new school up and running, as well. The town is definitely growing in a west direction. There's a mini library in the new playground area and I stopped as I went past it and wrote in my notebook, "When I publish my book, I will put a few copies here for people to read." As I walk farther out west along the path I come to the leading edge of town. One side of the path is houses and the other side is a field with a wonderful view of the mountains on a sunny day. I have seen many amazing sunsets from this path. As I walked on I stopped again and wrote down, "The trees and houses are on the leading edge and so am I because I have done so much changing and growing over the past three years and just like the trees and town, I will continue to grow and change."

Journal entry (11th) - Sunday again! We went to the Calgary zoo today with the whole family to celebrate Mother's Day. Zach LOVED the new penguin enclosure. They did a great job getting the zoo back up and running after the flood this spring. That must have taken a lot of hard work and a lot of people. Co-creating at its finest. We also LOVED the Butterfly Garden. It was so humid and relaxing in there as the butterflies came and landed on us, it completely brought us to the present moment where there was no problem, only LOVE. You could feel the souls of all the captivating butterflies. This place made the whole day really worth it for me. Fun, fun with family. I also got lots of hugs today. Bet you didn't know that hugs are VERY important for our well-being. Cutaneous deprivation, also known as the lack of touch, leads to a host of emotional, physical and developmental problems in young and old alike. So do lots of hugging.

Also I said to someone, who I thought was a friend, that I was thinking about writing a book. She replied, "You'll never do that! You're going to make yourself sick again." I thought to myself, if this person who spewed all this negativity actually knew me at all, they would have surely pointed out all my other faults as well. I will be distancing myself from her because I choose to surround myself with loving, encouraging, inspiring, positive friends.

And one more story. No makeup, out in public, being my authentic self and tired because I had stayed up for a large portion of the night working on some writing that was flowing through me and I was getting groceries, which is something I do lots, with two growing boys. I was walking around in the produce section, checking out the broccoli and organic lemons. They have a great produce section at our local Co-op grocery store and my friend who works there saw me and stopped working to say hello. He asked me how it was going and I said, "Great! I'm writing a book". He paused and looked at me and said, "Oh... thanks for telling me. I was wondering if maybe you decided to start smoking pot. Your eyes are so red!" Funny Dave. I burst out laughing and was still smiling when I went through Melisa's till, whom by the way has my store number memorized. Half the people who work there know me on a first name basis. I love my small town community.

Reflect – What brings you joy? Do that today.

June - EASE

Yes, ease and flow. I have an Easy Button from Staples and use it often. Life is supposed to be easy and flow with only a little resistance. We just need to follow the steps that are needed for success. Zach was playing with his Electronics Lab kit one day and he was creating a light telegraph. I asked him what he was holding and he informed me that it was a super conductor and that it has zero resistance but only at a sub-zero temperature. He also filled me in that every material has some resistance. He then showed me a transistor and a 470 microfarad capacitor and told me that it holds electricity. I was told that if he gets one wire out of place then nothing works because the electricity can't flow because he has to follow the directions and take it one step at a time. Love my little science guy.

Keep on climbing up that emotional scale. It is so worth it. Zach and I each put our left hands on our hearts today then we joined our right hands together. We stared into each other's eyes until we burst out laughing. Try it. It's fun to connect with yourself then to connect with another. After we were done laughing, I said to Zach, "I see you," and he replied, "I see you too!"

Water. Drink lots of good water. It's great for detoxifying. You could drink it with green tea or with lemon and honey and other great foods that have a detoxifying effect are: cucumber, garlic, broccoli, lentils, greens, seeds, nuts, turmeric, citrus fruit, watercress, mung beans, artichoke, dark chocolate covered almonds and whole grains. Be wary of what you put in your body. I also discovered when I was sick with my dis'ease' that it takes very little to sustain our bodies. It's okay to cut back on portion sizes. You will be just fine. You are what you eat.

One of the girls in my class said to me today that words are like wool and that books are like cloth. She explained that you need wool to make cloth and you need words to create a book. I agreed and also added that if we use good wool then our cloth will be better. She smiled.

Journal entry (9th) - What a great day for a massage with Jodi. I always feel so connected and balanced and relaxed and focused after a visit with her. Thanks Jodi, today I feel unsinkable. You're so full of light and love.

Open up the blinds and let the light in. I did my Pilates in a sun puddle today. It was great and I felt even better after than I usually do. I was really in the moment and nothing was going to distract me. I had completely shut off the monkey mind. I was trusting in myself and listening to my body. No mind chatter. I relaxed into it and let the resistance go and each time I stretched I found I could go a little farther. I felt like Frisco who also loves stretching in a sun puddle.

The boys and I were visualizing today. Jaden sees himself getting accepted to college, a brand new 4X4 truck and a job that he loves, which also brings him lots of money. Zach sees himself working at CERN (European Centre for Nuclear Research) as a physicist of maybe doing science on the ISS (International Space Station) of maybe both. He also sees himself playing his trombone and having the 'dad experience'. I see a few family trips in our future. One trip to China to walk on the Great Wall and one to an all-inclusive resort in Mexico and I've always wanted to go to Hawaii. When I was a young girl our family would go to the interior of BC every summer. I want to recreate that trip with the boys. I want to stay at Canyon Hot Springs Resort then drive into the Okanagan and spend some time there. I see a new exercise bike and also, a purple/pink 4X4 Jeep so that I never get stuck in the back alley again. I saw a cool paintjob the other day and depending on how you looked at the car it was purple or pink - so cool. It was all about which angle you looked at it from. And of course I see dark chocolate covered almonds and lots of them.

Sunday again! Zach and I are going to start a Happiness Box in the New Year. Every night before bed we'll write about something from the day that made us smile or laugh or even just something we are grateful for and then we will be able to fall asleep with positive thoughts on our minds and have sweet dreams. Then at the end of the year or on days when we are feeling low on the emotional scale we can pull out the papers and read again all about our wonderful things to help bring us back up.

It was an awe inspiring day as Deer Meadow had their triathlon. Zach was the swimmer, Chris was the biker and Navi was the runner for their trio. I was the swimmer, Dakota was our biker and Jenna was our runner. Life just keeps getting better and better.

This pretty much sums up the school year. Bailey wrote to me, on Facebook - "Thank you Ms. Taylor for the best year ever and thank u for the best class video of us over the year!! You and Mrs. Clarke were amazing!! Thank you"

I'm looking forward to an awesome summer holiday with the boys. Fun! Fun! Fun!

Reflect - Some doors in your life open with ease. Describe one such door.

July - APPRECIATION

July is my month of appreciation. This emotion is big in my life. Gratitude has created miracles for me. I make it a habit to appreciate all people and things. I appreciate them fully and sincerely without any expectations. When I truly appreciate life then life is so much more full and beautiful.

Feeling particularly grateful for dad. I come from strong genetic material. We take a kicking and keep on ticking. I'm feeling grateful that he's still in my life. Dad has had many setbacks in his life and always bounces back stronger. The one I'm thinking of now, is when he was run over by a tractor and ended up on the other side of the large back tire. Dazed and confused he crawled to the house to get help and called mom, who called the ambulance. He said he remembers his dog, Shady, licking his face to keep him going. The ambulance driver said that they thought they had lost him a couple times on the trip to the city. He spent quite a few months in the hospital recovering from this one - broken ribs, broken pelvis, internal bleeding and a broken leg. Dad has also struggled with other medical conditions on and off all his life. He has demonstrated incredible courage as he jumped some very scary hurdles of his own.

I was looking at pictures today of a lake that we love to hike around to get to a waterfall in Kananaskis Country and I thought to myself - the lake is calm on the surface and I bet it's calm deep down too. There is so much oneness and everything is so connected. I feel so in the flow when I'm in nature.

I was relaxing in the backyard today in the hammock and doing a Sudoku when I looked up and got lost in the beauty of the sky.

It was a perfect day with a bright blue sky containing all kinds of white fluffy, floating shapes. I spent some time, not sure how much because I got lost in the beauty and time stood still, looking at shapes and forms. I definitely saw some hearts and feathers up there and many other things that transformed before my eyes. What an amazing world we live in!

Zach was watching *Kung Fu Panda* and as I walked in the door, the wise old turtle named Master Oogway on his movie said, "Yesterday is history, tomorrow is a mystery, but today is a gift. That is why it is called the present." I believe this message was for me and that it wasn't just a coincidence. I said the same thing at grandma's funeral in my speech for her and I think it was her giving me the message back. Actually I've been getting lots of messages lately and now believe that there is no such thing as coincidence. So anyway, this was cool because I had just walked in the door from a drive which I needed to take because I knew I needed to scream and cry and I didn't want the boys to see that. I went and did my thing. Tears rolled and I yelled into thin air for quite some time then it just stopped and I started laughing so hard that the tears continued to roll but they had a whole new feeling. Then a feeling of calm came over me as I looked in the rear view mirror and said to myself, "I guess I left that behind." I stared at the mountains on the horizon and decided to turn around. I turned on the radio and the song, "I Get Knocked Down" by Chumba Wumba came on and I sang at the top of my lungs all the way home. By the time I walked back in the house I was all smiles again. I realized that it didn't matter what was in the mirror or what was on the horizon I was needing to let some negativity inside go so that I could be happy in this moment. And it was also funny because the guy who passed me stared at me like I was a crazy lady then his stare turned to a smile as he went by. Yup, we are all a little crazy.

July has been a great month for letting go of stuff and also cleaning house. I've washed every wall and window in the house and I have a huge pile of stuff in the garage that I'm donating to the

Canadian Diabetes Association. It feels good to de-clutter and then share the stuff we no longer need.

Also, great news! Jaden has manifested wheels now. A beat up old truck but that's ok because it will still get him where he wants to go. So excited for all the new adventures he's going to have with it. I promised him that I won't yell, "BRAKES! BRAKES! BRAKES!", if I go for a drive with him.

Reflect - What are you grateful for? Make a Gratitude Wheel.

August - EMPOWERMENT

Empowerment comes from within and I have made great gains in this emotion. I have always known that confidence was important and as I went down the cancer road I faced powerlessness on many occasions, especially during chemo, and I dug deep to release that negative emotion. This month I look back and I feel empowered to live the best life I can. I'm confident that I can achieve that.

I walked around my house today and took pictures of all kinds of "stuff" that is in my house. Then I downloaded the pictures and looked at them on the computer. It was so cool because I saw my same old things in a new and more angelic way. It was about seeing them from a new perspective. I appreciate all that I have and I take nothing for granted today.

Played Scrabble with Zach and I started to think about all the words that end with 'ire'. Here are some I wrote down. Sure-fire. Inspire. Admire. Transpire. Desire. Conspire. Campfire. Cheshire. Sapphire. Acquire. Enquire. Haywire. Require. Expire. Vampire. Attire. Empire. Retire. Aspire. Overtire. And Billionaire! ☺ So being the teacher that I am, I couldn't leave it at that. I went to www.merrian-webster.com/dictionary/ire and discovered that it meant intense and usually openly displaying anger. That didn't jive with me so I read on to discover that the obsolete, old fashioned and archaic meaning of the word means 'mood'. That worked for me. Sometimes older is better. With age comes wisdom. Nan would agree.

I have decided to do the Gratitude Challenge on Facebook. For five days, I choose three things that I am grateful for. This is going to be fun. I was nominated by Alissa to do the Five Day Gratitude Challenge. Why is gratitude a good thing? Thinking about what is right in your world puts you in a state of love. The sincere moments of appreciation are in complete alignment with who you are. It is a wonderful thing to hold something as your object of attention while you feel that appreciation within yourself. It makes a full circle and gives the appreciation momentum that takes you into higher and higher places. So let's go higher and higher. I challenge you.

Day One

1) I am grateful for Jaden who makes me laugh and smile every day. He demonstrates determination and perseverance. He is strong and quiet and he has been there for me more than anyone could possibly know. He is wise and mature beyond his years.
2) I am grateful for Zach who is my biggest teacher. He inspires me to look deeper at things because there is always more to know. My little scientist/trombonist/football player who has a heart full of love and isn't afraid to be himself and live from his heart.
3) I am grateful for this beautiful house full of love that I call my home.

I nominate Sheila, Janet and Wendy to write 3 things you are thankful for, for 5 days and nominate whoever you want.

<u>*Day Two*</u>

Great things come in 3's for me!

1) I am grateful for my mom (Sheila) because mom flipped upside down says wow and that is what she is to me.
2) I am grateful for my sister (Janet) because she is always there for me. Through the laughter and the tears.
3) I am grateful for my sister (Wendy) because she inspires me to step out of my comfort zone and grow.

Reflect - What makes you feel empowered and confident?

September - FREEDOM

T he butterfly on my tattoo symbolizes freedom and the beauty that comes from finding it. I also believe that the valleys in life are where we can find our freedoms but that we don't always have to go through darkness to see the light. I also think that sometimes darkness is necessary for change to happen. I know it was for me. It's a good idea to learn from others, as well, because life is too short to make all the mistakes yourself.

Today I am free to feel grateful.

Day 3 of my Gratitude Challenge. (Inspired by spending the day at the farm with family).

1) I am grateful for my dad (Don) who has shown me that obstacles can be overcome and that '$h!t happens - deal with it and move on' and for my Step mom (Irene) who helps keep dad grounded and calm when '$h!t happens'.

2) I am grateful for all my extended family. I see unconditional love when I look at you. Perry and Mike (my brother-in-laws) and all my nieces and nephews (Alex, Riley, Jaxon, Nate, Maddy and Mia). Also my cousins, aunts and uncles.

3) I am super grateful for my good health right now - enough said.

Day 4 of my Gratitude Challenge and the first day back to school. New beginnings are fun. I know it is going to be an amazing year! (Jaden - grade 12 and Zach - grade 6).

1) I am grateful for friends. I am so blessed to have so many who live near and far. I'm a lucky girl! So I guess I am also grateful for the computer and internet so I am able to connect with the ones who are far.
2) I am grateful for my job as a teacher. Love, love, love my job! And all the friends I have made through it.
3) Grateful for football. Fun, laughter and learning for our whole family. And all the friends I have made through it. Also grateful for my car to get us to the fun.

Day 5 and the final day of the Gratitude Challenge. Thanks again Alissa for the nomination.

1) I am grateful for abundance in all areas of my life.
2) My list of things that come to mind - Frisco, No-feet, sunshine, storms, dark chocolate covered almonds, my bed, nature, God, adventures, music, smiles, laughs, hugs, books, all our delightful seasons, mountains, beaches, Pilates, animals, living in a small town in Canada, long walks, meditation, food, red wine, tea, camping, backyard fires, stars, sunsets and sunrises, long baths, massages, movies, popcorn, snuggling with a blanket, skating, skiing, love.
3) I have so much to be grateful for and I am thankful for all that was, all that is and all that will be. Life is good and all is well in my world.

Rightness (Day-to-Day). School is back in and I'm on the sub list this year and days not subbing are being spent thinking about a book again. Both boys are doing football this season. Zach is a

Husky and Jaden is helping to coach the team. Jaden is a last year Spartan. Grade twelve and grade six. Seems like just yesterday they were in grades nine and three. This is going to be a fun year. Feeling Great. Loving Life. Bring It.

Well the Law of Attraction works fast for me. I am a great manifester. Yesterday mom forwarded me, an email from her friend Sue with the subject 'Do you have a Law of Attraction story?' mom typed to me, "Would you be interested in this? I'm not sure if I have anything yet." I typed back without any hesitation and it just flowed out...

"I attracted 2 beautiful baby boys, a house, a teaching career and on August 22, 2011 I attracted a divorce and breast cancer on the same day and today I attract great health, wonderful relationships and abundance in all areas of my life. Everything in my life I have attracted. The good and the not so good (but I do have to say that the not so good stuff gave me great growth)."

She replied...

"What a fabulous way to look at your life. I would love to have you included in my eBook, if you are willing to share the details. You could write it or I could interview you and write it. Let me know what works for you."

I slept on it and woke up excited and eager for the day. I exercised then did the sway test and the answer came back yes, so I write back...

"Hi Sue,

This sounds great. I would love for you to interview me. Just the other day, on Sept. 2nd, I wrote in my journal, "...thinking about a book again." It was a kid's book that I was thinking about but the thought did pop into my mind to write an autobiography too. I giggled to myself and thought - 'Yup, my life is a great story. It would make a great movie too' - LOA in Action ☺ We are great manifesters. The Universe has brought us together through mom. Ask-Believe-Receive...it works every time when I go forth with a positive attitude and let go of the resistance. It will be great working with you.

Thank you!

Carol

PS) Things happen in 3's for me. My marriage was unhappy for 3 years, 3 years for a divorce, 3 years to get healthy from cancer..... looking forward to the next 3 years, I see great things unfolding ☺"

Things are always working out for me and I will know the path when I see it. I'm staying in my happy place until the impulse to act is so powerful that I have to go. This is freedom.

Reflect - What words come up for you when I write the word freedom?

October - INSPIRATION

I gave myself my 'hour of power' this morning as I always do. It's so important for me to give myself that time to exercise and settle into the day before I go out there and have fun. This time fills up my inner self and helps me find inspiration in everyday events. When I'm stretching after I ride my bike, it is so cool, because as I relax into the stretch and breathe my body stretches even further. There are no torn muscles or forcing it to happen - just a relaxed stretch that feels good and takes me farther. There is a little resistance but not too much.

I was typing away the other day and then I saw the shift key and thought, Yes ... SHIFT. SHIFT? - the crazy and amazing things that go through one's mind as they are typing. I am going to have to dig into that one more.

Was going to get groceries and heard the song, "True Colors", by Cyndi Lauper. I listened to the words and realized how wonderful the song really is. She sang the words "beautiful like a rainbow" then I looked up and saw a bright and colorful sundog. The most colorful one that I had ever seen. It stopped me in my tracks as I stared at its beauty. Coincidence, I think not. If I had not been in the moment and aware then I would have missed this. Don't be afraid to let them show - your true colors.

I feel inspiration when I read this poem by G.Brian Benson. I read it to the kids at school and they like it too. They think that it would make a great kids book too. Thanks Brian!

We Are Meant To Succeed

Have you ever felt whiny, angry or sad?
Or tired and frustrated and then acted bad?
You're not alone, we've all been there before
When we're all out of sorts and acted quite poor

Take heart and take heed, it's the balance of life
Some days we're quite happy, others feeling some strife
The key to this game, is to understand how it's played
When you know what to expect, your confusion will fade

Love flows in balance, it's where we should be
Not too high, not too low, but the middle, you see
Be thankful and happy for where you are at
Life's here for learning, it's as simple as that

So during those times when it's tough or unsure
Take a step back and think thoughts good or pure
Remember a time when you had some success
Believe in yourself and never ever second guess

Your life is perfection, the good times and bad
The easy and the tough, the happy and the sad
Each challenge brings a chance to grow and become whole
To learn from mistakes, and reconnect with your soul

We are meant to succeed, so take heart and take flight
Throw out your fears and give way to love's light
Your destiny beckons, your true nature's at hand
Live life to its fullest, it's fantastic and grand!

Reflect - What inspires you? Now go do that.

November - AWE

S ue wrote my story. It's awesome! I sent it to Janice who is my lovely teacher/artist friend and she loved it too. She said I should expand on it. That is a great idea!

I experienced a chain reaction today at Tim Horton's. I was waiting for my tea and when I got to the window the nice lady said, "Here you go - your tea is paid for." Well that made my day, so I asked her how much for the order behind me and she said, "$11.47" and I gave her my debit card to pay for it. One person can make a difference but when many work together, watch out for miracles. I think of the pyramid effect too as I write this. I hug each of my boys as they go off to school, then they get to school and smile and do something nice for two people and then those two people pay it forward and so on and so on. Like I said, one person can make a big difference!

Journal entry (12th) - Just had the most relaxing bath with Epsom salts, baking soda and a drop or two of lavender oil. I completely cleared my mind and focussed on my breathing just for fun and I was so relaxed that I almost fell asleep in the tub. A bathtub meditation. Ah, life is good and water has such amazing healing properties.

Sunday again. It's 3:33 am and I woke out of a dead sleep with an urgent desire to write. This passage is coming from a complete place of stillness. I checked on the boys and they are both fast asleep. The house is quiet except for the running water in my fountain and the quiet hum of my furnace. Frisco hears me up and comes to check out what I'm doing. The moon is bright and the stars are out and the wild bunny has been here because I see its tracks in the snow. I stand there in awe for a while then I write: Believe me. When I was a single mom who was holding a divorce certificate, had no hair, was puking in the bathroom from the chemo, kids were arguing outside the bathroom door, kettle was whistling on the stove, laundry all over the living room, bills piled up on the desk, the cat just puked on the floor, I did NOT say, "Yes, I created this" but I look back now and see that YES, I did create that and if I can create that then I can also create good stuff. Let's start right now as I proclaim and you say it with me, "I am abundant in all areas of my life!" And don't just say it - FEEL it! And so it is. I love writing. Time just stands still when I am in that place of love.

Journal entry (24th) - I went to Stangs today for some multivitamins and some Pau D'arco tea. Perry is so knowledgeable and helpful. I love my small town!

Reflect - What is awesome in your life right now?

December - LOVE

This month I feel unconditional love in me and all around me too and I believe that love is what makes the ride worthwhile. All other positive emotions are focussed in love. All religions, songs, great stories of any kind also talk about this in great detail. You can find love in pretty much anything if you choose to look for it. This is the highest of the emotions on the emotional scale for me. The heart on my tattoo represents love because without love there is no life.

Zach and I were talking about how writing a book is like a band concert. Zach plays the trombone and loves it. We agreed that everybody needs to do their own part and do it well, which is a lot of hard work for each individual, then they come together in collaboration to make something bigger, better and more captivating. At the concert there is always wonderful music that inspires the crowd who are watching. Just like a good book too. Truly a team effort. We also agreed that great things need great leaders and Zach thinks that Mr. Wilson, his band teacher, would agree with that.

We have a wild bunny that comes around our house at night. I like the winter because when I wake up in the morning I can see if there are any new tracks from our wild friend. For the past few years we've been throwing carrots out under the cherry tree for him. When we see him on the rare occasion, we smile because to us he is a symbol of the freedom and beauty of nature and also he is a sign for us that all is well. In the winter he is white and in the summer he turns brown.

Zach started a new thing recently. He'll come and tuck me in at night and give me twelve kisses because he's twelve, then he'll give me three more and say with each on, "One for good luck. One for good dreams. And one for good luck with your dreams." He is so adorable!

Journal entry (25th) - Merry Christmas! Guess what! I got a lava lamp! It's even more mesmeric than the one I had been visualizing.

What a great year that was and 2015 is going to be even better. The boys and I stayed up to midnight and made tacos and drank sparkling raspberry apple juice in wine glasses. A fun celebration of cool things to come. In the New Year we look forward to some planned adventures like Jaden graduating and either heading off to college or out into the work world. I'm excited about a Zip lining adventure that I'll be having with Team Believe as we raise money for cancer and make a fun, new memory. I also plan to continue on my book adventure and learn lots along the way. This book is like my third baby. I've poured my heart and soul into it and now I get to watch it go out into the world and fly but I keep reminding myself that good things take time. You wouldn't want to have the baby the day after it was conceived and in the same way, I know that this new journey will take time to manifest. Ask then believe and it will come. Plus once you put the idea out there, the universe conspires to make it happen and it adds extra good stuff as well to surprise and delight you. New friends come with new adventures!

I feel like an Alchemist who has transmuted hate, blame, anger, resistance, worry, guilt, depression and fear to joy, acceptance, passion, happiness, hope, excitement, trust and love! Things are not good or bad, they just are. It depends on your belief about the thing.

I look back now and see that my bucket was empty and that it was a good thing because that meant that I had lots of room for all the new, good stuff that I have learned. I am aware now that I can create my own life.

Feel Good - Give Thanks - Trust

Live - Love - Laugh - Let Go

Look - Listen - Learn - Lead

Love + Trust = Growth, Beauty and Freedom

Remember to breathe! 3-4-5

My bucket is full and it is time to give back!

I am thinking of my fellow warriors today. I could name at least 33 of you. I Love You!

Reflect - What make you feel unconditional love? What makes your heart sing? Make a love wheel in the shape of a heart.

Thanks for Coming

I hope you enjoyed coming along on my journey, from FEAR to LOVE. My hope is that you cried some inspired tears and read something that will help you on your journey. I hope your book is highlighted and scribbled in. If that happened then my work of writing this book feels complete. If you loved the book as much as I loved writing it then give it to someone else who needs it. Pay it forward. With that said I would like to share "My Tools" with you. In the November Chapter I mentioned that Sue wrote my story and she called it "The Toolbox" so I felt it appropriate to share the list of tools that I have accumulated. They are the things that bring rightness to my world. The things that move me up the emotional scale. My toolbox is always changing. I get rid of tools and I'm always adding new ones. Sometimes I lend them out and often friends will give me new ones. It's a continual flow of change. If you want to borrow tools then I am more than willing to share. Take what works for you.

My Tools

Ask	Align	Allow	Achieve	Accept	Activity	Apples
Animals	Adventure	Act	Appreciate	Angels	Authenticity	Adapt
Abundance	Almonds	Awareness	Believe	Beauty	Breathe	Birds
Baking Soda	Begin	Be Yourself	Butterflies	Bananas	Balance	Bravery
Be Present	Broccoli	Bath	Create	Choose	Confidence	Clouds
Change	Courage	Commit	Connect	Candles	Chocolate	Care
Cards	Cherries	Collaboration	Clarity	Communicate	Community	Cook

Clean	Compassion	Curiosity	Determination	Dedication	Duct Tape	Dream
Desire	Dance	De-clutter	Dandelions	EFT	Exercise	Ease
Eat well	Education	Epsom salts	Essential oils	Empathy	Emotions	Energy
Enthusiasm	Excitement	Focus	Fun	Family	Friends	Fire
Freedom	Flowers	Fresh air	Facebook	Feathers	Forgiveness	Faith
Flexibility	Give Thanks	Growth	Generosity	Gems	Goals	Hugs
Happiness	Honey	Hammer	Health	Healing	Harmony	Hearts
Imagine	Intuition	Joy	Kaizen	Know	Kindness	Kids
Lava lamps	Live	Love	Laugh	Let go	Look	Listen
Learn	Lead	Lemons	Leap	Mountains	Meditate	Movies
Massage	Memories	Manifest	Nature	Namaste	Oranges	Ocean
Prevention	Prepare	Passion	Pleasure	Peace	Perseverance	Pilates
Plants	Pure water	Positive	Purpose	Popcorn	Plan	Play
Question	Quad	Rainbows	Respect	Reflect	Receive	Relax
Research	Romance	Stillness	Surrender	Success	Sleep	Stars
Sunshine	Screwdriver	Share	Sing	Smile	Soup	Ski
Salt lamps	Simplicity	Satisfaction	Strength	Spirituality	Teamwork	Try
Trust	Take pictures	Tea	Turmeric	Tranquility	Understand	Unique
Visualize	Value	Vitamins	Vitality	Vacuum	Walk	Words
Water	Warmth	Wellness	Worthiness	Wisdom	Xenia	Yoga
YouTube	Yogurt	Zen				

I end this book by saying that I've discovered that it's ALL right. What will the future bring? I don't know and I'm okay with that. I'll figure it out as I go and so will you. Thank you so much for coming on this journey with from Fear to Love with me! Without you it would not have been the same. Where there is love, there is beauty. Much Love and Light to you!

(((HUGS))) & Smiles ☺
Carol

(P.S) Remember… It's ALL right!

For Your Thoughts

"We are all here to learn about ourselves and
inspire others in our own unique way."
~ G. Brian Benson ~

Acknowledgements

As I was writing the journal entries for this book, I felt the joyful, solitary creation of just the Universe and myself, as the words flowed through me. When I accumulated all my writings, I experienced wonderful healing as I looked back and kept moving forward. There were many days that I had to stop typing because I was getting tears on the keyboard. Then my circle started to grow and got bigger and bigger and more people joined the circle until there were many people. They have all contributed to the creation you now hold. Feeling so grateful!

Thank You and (((HUGS))) & Smiles to...

My family, friends and community. All the pages of this book are filled with acknowledgments to the thousands of incredible souls who were a vital part of the creation of this story and book. I acknowledge every one of you in this limited space. Thank you for blessing my life with your unconditional love and support and know that a tribute to each of you lives on in my soul forever. Without you this story would not be possible!

My boys for their constant love, warm hugs and sticky fingers. Jaden for the 'Smiling Single Mom' Logo and his technical support and graphic abilities as I learned to design webpages, Twitter, Pinterest, blog and skype. Zach for compassion and generosity on an everyday basis and for bringing up my feel good hormones with a large dose of dopamine and serotonin.

Janice Gallant for enriching my story with her stunning painting. Her art is a reflection of her beautiful soul. Also for her help with editing and publishing, but most of all thank you for sharing my dream. I am your biggest cheerleader as I know you are mine. You can see more of her work at http://www.janicegallant.com/.

Sue Methuen for writing "The Toolbox" which inspired me to do some writing of my own. Thanks also for the many links that she shared with me about self-publishing. She is a kind, patient person who was a joy to work with. I recommend that you check out her other pieces of writing at http://www.simplechanges.ca/books

Sheila Page for the cover photo. My Mom and one of my best friends! This picture was taken on a bike ride we took to the country on a captivating fall day. It was a magical moment. Mom upside down is Wow and that is what she is to me. Love you forever!

G.Brian Benson for his poems, books, emails, quotes, kind words, encouragement, intuition, positive caring vibes and for being a dear friend and a true beacon of light to me. His work and personality has always resonated with me. You can view his website at http://www.gbrianbenson.com/ . He is also on Facebook as G. Brian Benson.

Steve Taylor for his poem, "Become the Sky". His work is truly inspiring and exquisite and it is a meditation just reading his words. He is a teacher in the true sense of the word. His website is http://www.stevenmtaylor.com/ Check out his new book, *The Calm Center*. You can also find him on Facebook.

Abby Dalton for her poem and her amazing personality. She believed in me even when I stopped believing in myself. She is a multi-talented leader who will go far in this life. Her energy lights up my life.

Gerald Rogers for his poem, "Courage" and for just being an all-round great guy. His work is magnificent and so is his personality. He is a Smiling Single Dad. You can view his website at http://geraldrogers.com/. He is also on Facebook as Gerald Rogers.

Chantal Thorburn for the author photo. I met Chantal in prenatal classes and now our boys are graduating together. We meet people for a reason and I am grateful that I have had her in my life. She is a soul SiStar.

Patricia for her editing expertise, services, wonderful suggestions and friendship. Collaboration at its finest! The universe conspired to bring us together! She helped me to see that my story was all about the rightness of my situation.

Balboa Press for their help with Editing, Production and Distribution. Without them this book would not be in your hands today. Ever grateful for this team of amazing people! Boy, there was a lot to learn here and they made the process SO much easier!

The Alberta Writers Guild for reading my manuscript and giving me feedback so that I could make it even better. It was real nice to have some fresh eyes give me feedback. Thanks!

My medical support team who I was so blessed to be put in the hands of. Dr. Ebeth Hoffman, my family doctor, at the Wild Rose Health Clinic. She cried with me and laughed with me. Dr. Tsang and a nurse named Nicole and all the people at the Tom Baker Cancer Centre at Foothills Hospital in Calgary. Nicole blew up a surgical glove and gave it to Zach as a balloon, at the appointment when Zach came with me. Dr. Mew, my focused, conscious surgeon. I always felt that God had me placed in their hands for a good reason.

"It's about people and how much we really have in common"
~ G. Brian Benson ~

How To Find Me

To Get In Touch With Carol...

you can...

Email her at taylorc@live.ca

or

to follow her blog or order additional copies
of Smiling Single Mom for yourself or a friend,

go to her website <u>www.smilingsinglemom.ca</u>

Recommended Reading Resources

For You

Brian's List by G .Brian Benson
The 5 Love Languages by Gary Chapman
Feel the Fear and Do It Anyway by Susan Jeffers
Waking From Sleep by Steve Taylor
The Christmas Secret by Donna VanLiere
The Book of Awesome by Neil Pasricha
You Can Heal Your Life by Louise Hay
Ask and It Is Given by Esther Hicks
Positive Discipline by Jane Nelson
Meditation for Beginners by Jack Kornfield
The Alchemist by Paulo Coelho
Don't Sweat the Small Stuff with your Family by Richard Carlson
Laughter is the Breast Medicine by Eileen Kaplan
Manifest your Destiny by Wayne Dyer
Chicken Soup for the Breast Cancer Survivor's Soul by J. Canfield, M. V. Hansen and M. O. Kelly
Stillness Speaks by Eckhart Tolle
The Marriage Advice I Wish I Would've Had by Gerald Rogers

For Kids

Love You Forever by Robert Munsch
Artemis Fowl Series by Eoin Colfer

My Favorite Things by Lori Clarke
I Knew You Could by Craig Dorfman
I Love You the Purplest by Barbara M. Joosse
All the Places to Love by Patricia MacLachlan

About Carol

A small town girl, Carol grew up in Central Alberta on a farm just west of a small rural community. She is the oldest of three girls. After graduation she moved to Olds with her future husband. They were together for twenty six years and in that time they co-created two marvelous boys and a lot of wonderful memories. Carol had a variety of jobs, but enjoyed her work as a lifeguard & swimming lesson instructor and her work at the daycare the most. She has always loved working with children. This inspired her to get her Bachelor of Education in 1995. She is currently an active teacher in her small town. She was routinely doing her monthly breast exam in July, 2011 when she discovered a lump in her right breast. After going through a mastectomy and chemotherapy, she decided that her body had been through enough and listened to her heart which told her that radiation and drugs were not needed and she should focus on her healing. She enjoys spending time with her boys, going on adventures, writing, reading, cooking, hiking, biking, living in the moment, loving, laughing, learning, drinking tea, meditating, doing Pilates, Facebooking, eating dark chocolate-covered almonds, spending time in her yard and in nature. Currently she is teaching part time so she can spend time on her new adventure of writing. She is passionate about expressing herself in words that inspire and bring hope to others who experience the process of cancer or any other learning experience actually. She believes a positive attitude can create miracles. Keep a look out for future works.

About Janice

J anice is a teacher, illustrator and artist living in Central Alberta, Canada with her husband and two dogs. She offers fine art paintings in oils and watercolor and also illustrates and writes children's books. Inspiration for her work comes from her own experiences raising three children, teaching her middle school students, and the surrounding beauty in nature.

She first learned how to create art with oil paints when she was twelve years old from her talented father, Ross Pritchard. Growing up in the family business, an art gallery and picture framing store allowed her to be surrounded all her life with many great artists and to learn many different techniques from several different artists. She creates in pencil, pen & ink, oils, watercolors, and acrylics. Her style is unique with lots of movement and vibrant colors, expressing energy in her work. Her study of art and famous artists such as Ted Harrison, the Group of Seven, Emily Carr and many others have all had an influence on her developing her own unique style.

She expresses, "We live in a world of color, energy and movement and I hope my paintings depict this along with inspiring your emotions in a wonderful way. Living in Alberta, I am continually inspired by the nature, the scenery around me."

Visit her website at www.janicegallant.com

Printed in the United States
By Bookmasters